Is He?

Is He Cheating?

By

Aileen Christine

This book is a work of non-fiction. Names and places have been changed to protect the privacy of all individuals. The events and situations are true.

First published by AuthorHouse 05/21/04

ISBN: 1-4184-6346-9 (e-book)
ISBN: 1-4184-4808-7 (Paperback)

Library of Congress Control Number: 2003095854

Printed in the United States of America
Bloomington, Indiana

This book is printed on acid free paper.

Dedication

This book is dedicated to the special men and women who have desperately fought, or are fighting to save their marriage, although their partner has already filed for divorce.

A special thanks to Almighty God for His unfailing love and giving me victory. May all the Glory be His.

Also to family members who prayed and supported me.

Acknowledgement

In memory of my father, Artist Bill J. Markowski, who fell ill during my time of adversity. I will always remember his advice. "It's another chapter in your life, turn the page," he would say. It was not until after he passed away, that I discovered a small watercolor painting that he had sketched of my ranch, which is being used for the cover design.

A special thanks to poem writer, Gary J. Silva for all the hours he spent supporting me.

Introduction

The book is based on a true story. It explains the type of suffering one experiences when discovering that their marriage partner is having an affair. Divorce always brings pain and suffering. It hurts, especially if you are the rejected partner. The story explains how my desperation to save my marriage led me to make the wrong decisions. The story also tells how trusting in God through prayer and perseverance led me to victory.

Ryan and I were married for nine years and we had always considered our marriage a happy one. I never thought that one day my husband would jeopardize his marriage, family life and everything he had just to satisfy his lustful desires to be with another woman.

The book also explains some of the signs that I observed in my husband's behavior while he carried out his affair and prior to his leaving me on Christmas morning.

My husband was a police officer and I was a deputy sheriff. We both knew that law enforcement was a very risky profession, as well as stressful. I guess that's why it was easy for me to blame his job for his strange behavior. We both worked Monday through Friday and spent our weekends together with the boys. Ryan loved spending time down at his father's ranch. He would look after the cattle or go fishing for catfish down at the pond. His favorite pass time was hanging out at his best friend's ranch drinking beer and telling stories.

Ryan was handsome. He stood five feet eleven inches tall. He had broad shoulders and strong arms. His thick brown mustache matched his hair. My heart would skip a beat every time I gazed into his big green eyes. He was a lot of fun to be with, when he was in a good mood. Other times, he was quiet and grumpy and kept to himself. He was a good husband and I loved him very much, enough for me to accept and tolerate his grumpy quiet ways. The story tells how Ryan secretly became involved with another woman, and how one day with the help of his mistress, he plotted on leaving me on Christmas morning 1997, destroying our marriage and all of our dreams. The information you are about to read will give you an understanding as to why certain husbands act the way they do before they leave their wives. Some husbands carry out these behavioral signs just because of the type of person they are, and not because they are having an affair. It is just a matter of knowing your husband well enough to recognize the difference in his behavior. If you suspect that your husband is having an affair and he is portraying most of these signs, then chances are that he might be seeing another woman and is probably contemplating leaving you soon.

After our divorce, I discovered that Ryan was involved in more than just one affair. I never suspected that Ryan would even see another woman. He was always so quiet and his constant reassurance that he was not seeing another woman convinced me to trust him.

I remember one year as a child, I received a little red barn with plastic farm animals for Christmas. I would play for hours with my farm animals and dreamt that one day I would own my own real farm. Then one day my dream came true.

I was a single parent raising three children when I was hired at our local sheriff's department. I went through the academy and was certified as a deputy sheriff. It was there at the academy that I met Ryan. He was sent by his agency to train with our Gang Unit officers. We started dating and fell in love. Several months later we were married. Six months later, I discovered that I was pregnant. I was reassigned to the captain's office typing and filing reports until I gave birth to our son. When baby Tyler was three months old, I was transferred to the county courthouse where I performed as a Bailiff. After the baby's first birthday, Ryan eagerly drove us out to the country and surprised us with a beautiful ranch house on twelve acres, which he was planning to buy. Well, we were excited and I knew that my childhood dreams were about to come true. We bought the ranch and moved in. I had always strived to be a good housekeeper and worked hard at cleaning, fixing, sewing and decorating the house. I wanted that warm cozy country atmosphere that I had dreamt about for so long. A few months later the farm animals started arriving. We had cattle, chickens and one little bunny named Star. I enjoyed the many afternoons watching Ryan out in the field working the cattle, while I tended to the housework and cooking. Washing dishes was not just a chore for me, it was an opportunity for me to relax, meditate and pray. I enjoyed looking out the kitchen window watching the birds and cats up on the deck as they played and teased each other.

Other times, I dreamt about Ryan and I growing old together with the kids all grown up and coming around with the grandchildren. So many happy thoughts roamed my mind. I was happy and felt complete for the first time in my life. I wondered what I had done to deserve such a blessing. But how little did I know that those dreams would soon be destroyed, changing my life and the lives of our children forever.

When Ryan was transferred to the night shift, we hardly saw each other. We had to adjust our schedules and find ways to make time for each other. One night, he came home early from work and sadly informed me that he had responded to a burglary in progress and killed a man. The burglar shot at Ryan several times and Ryan shot back stopping him with a single shot to the chest. He was pretty shook up about the incident and was placed on administrative leave pending the investigation. Two weeks later he was cleared of the incident and was given orders to return for duty. Ryan declined offers to seek counseling and convinced everyone that he was fine. Toward the last two years of our marriage, Ryan started seeing another woman. She was the night shift manager for a small convenience store located in town.

During his affair, Ryan would come home and criticize my manner of housekeeping. Why would he tell me these things? He criticized me this way because he was guilty of his affair. By convincing himself that I was a lousy housekeeper or cook, it made it a whole lot easier for him to justify his reasons for seeing the other woman.

Ryan and I kissed a lot. We kissed good-bye and we kissed hello, just like most married people do. I would look forward to Ryan coming home from work just so I could give him that warm hello kiss. During the last year of our marriage our kisses became fewer and fewer, up to the point where he wouldn't let me kiss him anymore. My heart would sink with pain when he would turn his face away from mine, only allowing me to kiss him on the cheek. He had probably just finished kissing the other woman before coming home and felt guilty kissing me. His lips were tainted from her kisses, which is probably why he would turn his face away.

Why would he suddenly ruin family plans? He always agreed with me to do something fun with the kids. But when the time came, he suddenly had to leave to take care of business, ruining our plans. This was very frustrating, since the boys and I looked forward to these events for days and then to just have them crash at the end. Sometimes, Ryan would leave the event early, or leave before we even got started because of the important thing he had to take care of suddenly. I know now that the only important thing that he had on his mind was going to see the other woman, who was probably jealous of our family plans and enticed him to come over to her place instead.

Ryan always stared at me with a big smile on his face making me feel loved and wanted. The last few months before he left, I noticed he would stare at me, but this time without a smile. A husband who is having an affair will sometimes stare at his wife with an expressionless look on his face. He is probably wondering if she has any indication about his big secret. Better yet, he might be trying to build up the guts to tell her he's leaving, or asking her for a divorce.

Are you always sitting next to an empty dinner chair? There are different reasons why a husband would be late for dinner. A sincere husband working overtime will usually pick up something to eat at work, or he will gladly eat what you had prepared for dinner that evening. Watch out if he comes home refusing to eat, or turns his face away when you try to kiss him. He probably finished having dinner and...*dessert*...at the other woman's home. Even if the mistress is a bad cook, she will always try her best to prepare better meals than the ones being prepared by you. This is her way of inviting him to spend time with her.

Why do some husbands want to sleep on the couch all the time? If he is sleeping with another woman, he will most likely choose to sleep on the couch, or in any another room. A cheating husband will feel unclean after enjoying a romantic sexual affair. The first thing he will want to do when he comes home is to take a shower and head for the couch. He won't want to sleep with his wife because of the inner shame and guilt that he is feeling.

Some husbands have no conscience at all and sleep with their wives anyway. Now, some husbands are either too lazy or too tired and innocently just fall asleep on the couch. So, please don't assume that he is having an affair and go pulling out the old rolling pin. If you know where your husband is at all times and he chooses to fall asleep on the couch, then chances are he is in love with that soft cushy couch of yours. But in certain cases, if your husband is showing any of the other mentioned signs in this book, then there might be a good chance that he is having an affair.

Does he pick on you for every little thing? Cheating husbands need to justify their reasons for seeing the other woman, and in doing so they will usually start a fight. They will look for ways to attack your manner of housekeeping, cooking, or just the way you handle the budget. Sometimes they will even accuse you of having an affair. So, once an argument starts, they begin to feel less guilty. Now they have a good reason to leave the house and run into the arms of their mistresses. This helps them to get away with their affair.

What about the phone calls? Are they slowing down or have they stopped all together? Are you finding yourself initiating most of the phone calls now? A cheating husband will usually lose his desire to call you at home or work. Why? He doesn't care anymore! He is too busy talking to the other woman in his life and spending his time thinking about her. This is a good indication that he might be having an affair. If your husband is a faithful loving man he will always try his best to keep in touch with you regardless of how busy he is.

Handyman or no handyman. He will still show a lack of interest on major or minor repairs. He no longer desires to fix or repair his home, like he once did in the past. He just doesn't care anymore. Usually, if he is asked to fix or repair something, he will do it in a hurry leaving a sloppy mess and the tools lying on the floor, before leaving the house and into her arms. The same sign applies if you are living in an apartment. His responsibilities decline when it comes to contacting maintenance, taking out trash or just helping with simple chores. His involvement in the affair will cause him to lose interest in his home.

A man will usually spend a lot of time day dreaming about the other woman. You will notice this a lot especially when he is seated in front of the TV set. When you notice him day dreaming, ask him a question about the movie that is being shown and see if he can give you an answer. After you break his trance, watch him as he tries to focus on the movie scrambling for an answer. This sign is usually a little harder to detect since it is impossible to know what he might be thinking. He could be thinking about work or a big project that he needs to present at work the following day. It's the unusual day dreaming that you need to keep an eye on. Watch him when he is unusually quiet.

Rejection is a good indicator. When a husband moves away from you or pushes your hand off his body, something is wrong. You will know something is not right when he starts to reject your love or gentle touch, especially in bed. He is experiencing new feelings for the other woman and does not desire your embrace or touch anymore. It's weird, because he feels that he is being unfaithful to her. You will definitely know something is wrong if he turns his lips away from yours and turns his back to you in bed. Usually, when you ask him what is wrong, he will simply answer that nothing is wrong or he is just tired.

Watch your husband as he leaves the house for work to see if he is taking extra clothes with him. If he is planning to see the other woman after work, he will probably want to change into something more comfortable. So watch for items like blue jeans, shorts, tee shirts and tennis shoes. Or, if he is planning to take her out, he will take something a little more than just casual. If you notice your husband carrying out extra clothes, ask him why he is taking them, or what his plans are after work. If he is seeing another woman, he will become defensive and answer rudely. Or, he will give you a logical answer to prevent you from suspecting his true plans. Try asking him to cancel his plans and come home immediately after work and see how he responds. Tell him you are planning something special for him and watch how he will try his best to wiggle out of it. If you don't see him carrying out any clothes and you suspect that he is seeing someone else, then you can always check his car prior to his leaving for work. Some husbands will sneak their clothes out ahead of time to prevent from being suspected. Now please don't mistake this sign if your husband is heading out to the gym or working a part time job. If your husband is faithful then you shouldn't have anything to worry about. Lots of men take extra clothing with them for certain occasions. I am talking about the sudden extra clothing that you need to watch out for, especially if it becomes a habit.

Dressing different is a good sign. Ryan always dressed in western attire. When he would come home from work, he wouldn't waste any time taking off his uniform and changing into a pair of jeans, western shirt and boots. Until one day he started wearing preppy polo shirts. Or, he would wear the little boy plaid short sleeve shirts. My one time macho rancher husband suddenly became a city boy. If your husband suddenly changes his style of clothing, then this might be a good indicator that the other woman is choosing your husband's clothes and convincing him to wear them for her own desires. Keep an eye on this one.

Less laundry is every woman's dream, but not when your husband's under garments are missing. Where are they? He left them at her place! Ask him where his articles are and see what kind of answer he will give you.

His haircut. This usually works if you have always been the one to cut your husband's hair. If the weeks are passing by and you notice that your husband's hair hasn't grown since the last haircut, then chances are that he is either getting his hair cut at the salon, or the other woman is cutting it for him. Try offering to cut his hair and see what he does. An unfaithful husband will sit there like a log with no expression on his face while you cut his hair. Try and kiss him and watch him tense up. This is a good sign, since you were used to him touching, teasing and playing with you during the haircut session.

Another good sign that your husband is planning to leave is when you start to notice certain items that belong to him are disappearing from the home. Slowly, a man will start transferring his items to the other woman's home or apartment. Conduct a walk through and randomly check your husband's closet, drawers and personal hygiene items to see if they are disappearing from their original place. Ask him where his stuff is and see what kind of answer he will give you.

Some husbands like to drink alcohol. When an unfaithful husband is planning to leave his wife, he becomes nervous and just the mere thought of leaving will lead him to drink more. So, keep an eye on his drinking and watch to see if it increases.

When a man is seriously planning on leaving his wife and family, he will not want to participate in family events. Such as Christmas, Thanksgiving or any other holidays. His mind is preoccupied with the evil intentions to leave his family. He is constantly deciding when would be the perfect time for him to make his big move. He will usually seclude himself from the rest of the family members and just sit around watching them as they enjoy themselves. Watch his facial expression when you ask him what is wrong. If he suddenly has to leave, then chances are that he is leaving and heading over to her place instead. Watch him as he leaves. Guilt will sometimes make a man turn and look back at you over his shoulder while he is walking away.

Most men love owning new cars or trucks. A faithful husband will usually take his wife with him shopping for a new vehicle. It's a special moment for both husband and wife when they choose a vehicle together and share in the excitement. Some husbands will purchase a new vehicle and bring it home to surprise the wife and kids. If your husband recently left the home and you discover that he suddenly purchased a new truck or car, then chances are that he has already left you for the other woman.

The new vehicle is to impress the other woman and to drive her around. An unfaithful husband is tricked by deception and will feel great for a short period. He will convince himself that he is doing the right thing. He begins to think that he is starting a new life by owning a new vehicle and having a new woman. But how little does he know that one day, he will find himself in for a rude awakening. When a man reaches this stage, he will usually go beyond his limits to purchase a new vehicle, even if he has to lie and persuade someone to co-sign or help with the down payment.

Your intuition is the best indicator that will lead you to believe, or suspect that your husband is having an affair. My mistake was ignoring my intuition, which repeatedly kept telling me that maybe my husband might be seeing another woman. I chose to ignore it, hoping that it was wrong. I strongly suggest that you listen to your intuition and take action immediately and investigate. I wasted a lot of time hoping Ryan would change on his own. I didn't start praying or trusting in the Lord until after Ryan left me. By then it was too late. The other woman had already devoured him.

Sarcastic Comments

One afternoon, I was busily wiping down the kitchen counters when I noticed Ryan standing near the kitchen doorway. He was leaning his body against the door frame and staring at me with a serious look on his face.

"Ryan, what's wrong?" I asked.

"You're a lousy housewife!" he blurted and then quickly walked away and headed toward his office.

A sharp little pain struck the center of my heart and traveled all the way down to the palms of my hands, as the smile slowly disappeared from my face. I stood still in the middle of the kitchen holding the dish rag in my hands, wondering what I had done to deserve such an insult. After Ryan locked himself in his office, I slowly walked around the house, looking and inspecting each room to see if I had missed an area that needed to be cleaned or picked up, but everything seemed to be in order. I couldn't understand what he was talking about and why he would call me a lousy housewife. I went back into the kitchen and continued with my chores, while keeping the thought in my mind.

"Maybe he's just having a bad day," I thought to myself.

I knew that when Ryan was in a bad mood, it was almost impossible to get him to talk about his problems. In the past, I had learned that it was best to leave him alone until he was ready to talk. His sarcastic remark kept torturing my mind. It seemed the more I cleaned, the more it invaded my mind. So, I stopped cleaning and went to bed. I was hoping he would come back and apologize or talk about his problem, but he didn't.

It was late in the afternoon and the boys and I were sitting at the kitchen table eating our dinner. The boys were quiet and I was depressed. I kept wondering where Ryan was and why he was late for dinner again. I looked up at the clock on the stove and noticed it was already 7:30 pm.

My eldest son, Isaac noticed that I had been glancing at the clock.

"Is dad going to be late for dinner again?" he asked.

"Yea, it looks like it son," I replied.

Once again, I had to convince the boys as well as myself that he was probably out at the ranch helping grandpa or his best friend Stanley. I slowly rose from my chair and began picking up the dinner dishes from the table when we heard the front door slam shut.

"Dad's home!" I announced to the boys.

The boys quickly jumped out of their chairs and ran out the back door. I stood near the kitchen table listening to the sound of Ryan's foot steps as he walked up the long hallway and toward the kitchen door. I looked up at him as he approached the doorway and noticed that he had that same serious look on his face. He just stood there staring at me. I wasn't sure if he had another bad day or if he was just upset with me. Feeling uncomfortable with his behavior, I smiled at him and tried to ignore the stern look in his eyes. I was just glad that he was home. I had been waiting for this moment where we could put our arms around each other and kiss each other hello.

As I began walking toward him, he quickly backed away and angrily blurted.

"You're a lousy cook! And you know what? I'm eating better than ever!" Ryan then quickly turned around and walked away.

I watched as he walked into his office locking the door behind him. Feeling hurt, confused and rejected, I slowly finished my chores and went to bed early. While lying in bed, I could feel the painful heaviness settling into my heart. *"Am I really that bad of a housewife and cook? And what did he mean that he was eating better than ever?"* I thought.

During the first seven years of our marriage, Ryan never insulted my cooking. Why now? Was he comparing my cooking to that of his mother's?

"Yes! That's it!" I thought to myself while forcing a sigh of relief.

I then turned and focused on the doorway of our bedroom with continuous visions of Ryan coming in and apologizing to me. I wanted so much for him to tell me that he didn't mean what he had said, but he didn't.

The Reassurance

One late evening, I was at the computer working on a project when Ryan quietly walked into the room. He had been gone all day and had missed dinner again. Feeling slightly nervous, I greeted him and then simply asked him where he had been.

"I was at a friend's house. You should be glad that I'm just with my friends. At least I'm not messing around with other women," he answered calmly.

Feeling secure and content with what he said, I rose from my chair and gave him a welcome home kiss. He stood motionless as I reached up to kiss his lips. His face was hard and cold like that of a statue. Ryan then pulled away from me and walked out of the room.

"Ryan! Do you want to eat?" I asked raising my voice.

"No! I'm not hungry," he answered while quickly disappearing into his office.

I thought about his answer and not realizing that I was gazing at the monitor's bright blaring screen.

"Why is he always telling me that he is not seeing another women. Is he?" I wondered.

While pondering the thought, I quickly convinced myself that everything was alright and ignored what might have been my intuition. Feeling confident that he was telling me the truth, I continued working on my project. Was Ryan telling me the truth? No, he wasn't.

One afternoon, I walked into Ryan's office and noticed that he was all dressed up in his hunting clothes and busily packing his gear.

"Is he going hunting again?" I asked myself.

I stood near the doorway of the office watching as he quickly packed his bags and aware that he was ignoring my presence. Ryan had been hunting a lot lately and was hardly ever home during the hunting season. There were very few times that Ryan would bring home a deer, hog or dove. The only time he brought something home was when he went hunting with his friend Stanley. I knew he was going hunting again, but…I don't know why, I had to ask him if he *was* going hunting again.

So, I asked Ryan the wrong question. You know, why he had to go hunting again. I knew I would be pushing the wrong button by asking that question. Well, I was right! Ryan quickly turned around and looked at me with an angry look on his face.

"Yea! I'm going hunting again! And you should be glad that I am not going out with another woman!" he yelled back angrily.

His sarcastic statement hurt, but it did convince me once again, that he was being faithful and that I should trust him. Forcing myself to believe that he was being faithful and not wanting to make a big fight out of it, I just exited the room. His harsh answer depressed me as well as having to face another long weekend by myself. I headed toward our bedroom and flopped face down on the bed. I could feel the cool breeze coming through the open window, comforting me as I thought about the long lonely weekend ahead of me. The bedspread felt so cool against my cheek as I lied there catching sight of the curtains twirl with the breeze. It almost appeared as if the curtains were dancing and trying their hardest to cheer me up. Then sadness crept upon me when I heard the sound of the truck's engine slowly sounding off in the distance. Ryan drove away without saying good-bye again. Visions of him turning the truck around and coming back raced through my mind. I wanted to kiss him good-bye and tell him that I loved him. I could have attempted to kiss him good-bye myself, but his quick departures were always unexpected.

"*Why was he always in such a rush to go hunting that he would forget to say good-bye to me*," I wondered. I kept staring at the open window hoping to hear the sound of his truck pulling back up into the driveway. I wanted so badly for him to return, but he didn't.

Turning His Face Away

I had already been insulted for being a lousy housewife, so I took it upon myself to work extra hard, spending the entire weekend cleaning the house. I wanted the house to look cleaner and neater than ever. Everything had to look great, so that when Ryan came home from hunting he would be pleased to find his castle clean. I even baked an apple cake for dessert. The entire time that Ryan and I had been married, he never insulted my looks. I always made sure that my hair was neatly combed and my face made up with just enough makeup to keep that natural look. Ryan never saw me sloppy and keeping myself well groomed always made me feel better about myself. So, he couldn't possibly be losing interest in me. So, I thought.

Well, it was late Sunday evening when he came in through the front door. I waited contently at the kitchen doorway where I would greet him. It felt good to know that he was home. When Ryan approached the doorway he looked at me with a big smile on his face.

"Hello Ryan," I said happily while greeting him.

I quickly walked up to him and put my arms around his neck and while I was reaching up to kiss him, I noticed his arms were hanging limp by his side. He smiled and slowly turned his face to the left, leaving me no choice but to kiss him on the cheek.

Then he quickly pulled away from me. He picked up his hunting bags and headed toward his office like usual. I stood there feeling dumb while the hurt worked its way through my heart.

"Why is he acting so strange? He wouldn't even put his arms around me," I thought to myself.

I walked over to his office and stood in the doorway watching him as he unloaded his bags, he was ignoring me again and I couldn't bear the silence any longer.

"Ryan, what's wrong?" I asked. He continued unloading his bags while ignoring my question. After asking him that same question several times and not getting an answer, I gave up and walked away feeling the edge of depression working its way through me.

"Is he…messing around?" I thought.

"No," I convinced myself out loud and headed back into the kitchen.

Again, he returned from his hunting trip without any deer, hog or dove. Not even a bug! I kept myself in the kitchen fiddling around suffering from feelings of disappointment and concern over his cold behavior. I was hoping he would follow me into the kitchen and sweep me into his arms and kiss me properly, but he didn't.

It was Thanksgiving Day! The kids and I were dressed up and ready to travel down to Aunt Carmen's house to celebrate the holiday. It was something we practiced every year. The boys were already outside impatiently hanging around the truck waiting to leave.

"Hurry mom, let's go!" yelled little Tyler.

"Ok, let me get your dad," I yelled through the screen door. I then hurried into the bedroom and found Ryan sitting on the bed with a serious expression on his face.

"What's wrong?" I asked.

"Nothing! Why don't you and the kids go on to your sister's house and I will catch up with you all later on," he suggested.

"Why?" I asked.

"I have something to take care of first," he answered. Well, I was surprised and disappointed in what he was suggesting. We always attended special events together as a family. Why did he all of a sudden have something to do now? Not wanting to argue or ruin a special day, I agreed with Ryan and quickly headed outside and loaded the boys into the truck. "Where's dad?" the boys asked.

"He had something very important to do again, he will catch up with us later," I answered.

Once we arrived at Aunt Carmen's house we joined the rest of the family who were sitting around the huge dinner table and having a great time. It seemed like the minutes were quickly flying by and Ryan still hadn't shown up yet. It just didn't seem right without him. Well, he showed up alright! A couple of hours later, after everyone had completed their Thanksgiving dinner. He walked straight into the dining room avoiding eye contact with me and began greeting some of the family members, while ignoring the rest of them who felt offended. Ryan didn't say a word to me, instead he just walked right past me and headed straight into the kitchen. I quickly got up from my chair and followed behind him.

"Do you want me to serve your plate?" I asked.

"No, I'm not hungry," he answered.

I smiled at him and wished him a Happy Thanksgiving. I then reached up to kiss his lips and he quickly turned his face away from mine. But this time he wasn't smiling. I immediately looked over his left shoulder toward where the family members were sitting, hoping they hadn't seen what had happened, or the hurt look on my face. This time I didn't kiss him on the cheek.

"What's wrong? Why are you acting so strange?" I whispered.

Ryan didn't say a word. He looked straight into my eyes while pulling himself away from me. He then quickly walked out the kitchen and headed for the front door. It almost looked as if he were running and I almost felt like fainting. I couldn't believe he was treating me like this. It was difficult trying to compose myself while enduring the tight pain in my heart. I felt panicky and quickly followed behind him smiling to family members pretending that everything was fine. I stopped on the porch and stood there like a statue as I watched him jump into his truck and leave. The heaviness in my heart felt like someone had hung a brick inside my chest.

"Why is he in such a hurry to leave? Where is he going? Is he mad at me?" All these questions raced through my mind in a split second. As I watched the truck disappear into the darkness, I prayed and hoped that he would come back, but he didn't.

Ruining Family Plans

It was the month of July and a hot one. Ryan and I had planned to take the boys to the coast the following weekend. The boys were really excited about going to the coast and began packing their bags right away. On Friday afternoon, I couldn't wait to get off of work. My mind was filled with things that I needed to take care of before heading out on our trip. I was so excited and relieved when five o'clock finally rolled around. I hurried to my truck and headed straight home. I quickly prepared dinner and began packing up the rest of our bags. It was already getting late and Ryan still hadn't come home for dinner. The boys and I ate dinner alone again.

"Where is he?" I wondered.

When Ryan finally came home the boys and I were fast asleep. On Saturday morning the kids and I were out of bed by eight o'clock. I was glad that all our bags were previously packed and ready to load up on the truck. I went into the bathroom to comb my hair and gather up a few items to take with me, and as I turned around to face the mirror, I was surprised to see Ryan standing near the doorway looking at me.

"I'll be right back, I have something I forgot to do!" he announced.

My fingers froze in my hair as I stared at my worried expression in the mirror. Naturally, I became distressed about his last minute errand.

"What?" I asked in a soft stunning voice.

"It won't take me very long and we will leave as soon as I get back," he assured me.

"What is it that you have to do?" I asked.

"I have to take care of some quick business, it will only take me a few minutes," he said.

He was amazedly patient and reassured me again that his errand wouldn't take very long, but somehow he always managed to get away by not telling me what he had to take care of all the time. I then pleaded with him to hurry so that we could get on the road. I stood by the bedroom window watching as he backed up the truck and drove away. Feeling uneasy about the whole thing, I turned and slowly sat on the bed.

"What is it with him? Why does he do these things?" I asked myself.

"Where is dad going mom?" the boys asked curiously.

"He'll be right back, he had something important to do," I answered.

Well, it started getting late and Ryan still hadn't come home. The boys were really getting anxious and continuously kept asking me when we were leaving. I had a sickening gut feeling that somehow this day was ruined and we were not going to the coast after all. It was already three thirty in the afternoon when I gave up on waiting for Ryan. I walked out onto the porch and sat down on the steps, watching and waiting to see if he would come home.

"Finally," I thought as I saw his truck coming up the road. He drove the truck into the driveway and

stuck his head out the driver window and yelled. "Let's go!"

"It's already four o'clock in the afternoon, it's too late," I explained yelling back. "Where did you go?"

"I was at a friend's house helping out!" he answered as he climbed the porch steps, disappearing into the house.

"*Yea sure,*" I thought.

I jumped up from the porch and followed Ryan into the house. The boys were sprawled out on the living room floor watching TV and didn't bother looking up at him as he walked past them. Ryan then stopped and looked at the boys. He suggested that we go anyway, but it was already too late. The boys were upset and I was hurt. I knew something was not right with Ryan and the only thing that I could figure out was that maybe the shooting incident had something to do with his behavior. The boys were disappointed and I felt sorry for them. They just hung around the house, while I sat in my old rocking chair feeling hurt and disgusted. Ryan didn't even seem to care that we were all depressed and just sitting around the house. Instead, he just sat in front of the old big TV ignoring the rest of us like it was no big deal. I just rocked and rocked in my chair while staring at the TV set. I couldn't help the visions of me just blowing away the TV screen with a single shotgun shell. I was hoping he would feel remorse for ruining our plans for the coast and at least apologize to the boys. Maybe he would offer to do something else, but he didn't.

One special Sunday morning my family and I had taken the boys to church to get baptized. Ryan was going to meet us at the church later that morning, since he had something to do again. This was a very special event for the boys and an emotional moment for me. I was in the back of the baptismal setting preparing the boys and filling out the necessary forms, when I noticed Ryan standing at the doorway. I was beginning to think that he enjoyed standing at doorways, right? Anyway, he just stood there like a statue not saying a word. Feeling uncomfortable with his behavior, I was afraid that he was getting ready to say something hurtful. So, I finished what I was doing and squeezed past him through the doorway.

"What's wrong with him?" I wondered as I quickly walked out of the room leaving him alone with the boys.

I felt guilty walking past him, since I always made it a habit to walk up to him and kiss him hello. This time I felt that it was best to not even try it. I then headed out to the sanctuary and joined the rest of the family. My family members sat on my right hand side while my in-laws sat to my left. Before the baptismal began, I noticed Ryan approaching the pew where we were sitting. He quickly scooted in and sat next to my father-in-law. I kept glancing at him wondering why he didn't sit next to me and still curious about his cold shoulder behavior. After the baptismal, we all gathered outside and began making plans to go eat and celebrate the special occasion. Ryan remained quiet the whole time ignoring me and the boys.

"Are you coming with us?" I asked looking directly into his eyes.

Somehow, I knew that he wasn't coming with us to celebrate. And I was right.

"No," he replied and quickly walked away without saying good-bye to me or any of the family members.

I watched him walk away. He stopped briefly just to look back at me and then kept on walking. I was hoping he would change his mind and come back to celebrate with us, but he didn't.

The Unusual Staring

I was excited! We were invited to a party at an old country bar in a small town just a few miles south of the ranch. I had been working hard all week and I was looking forward to attending the party. When Saturday arrived, we headed out to the party later that evening. While driving up the old bumpy dirt road we could hear the loud country music and the laughter of happy folks singing and dancing. Ryan then parked the truck along side the road. I opened the door and jumped out. I almost felt like a young little teenager all over again. I looked up into the dark sky and could see the millions of bright stars just twinkling above.

While standing there smelling and absorbing the cool breeze, I noticed that Ryan was already walking toward the bar. I then hurried to catch up to him and began walking along side of him. We didn't hold hands, since Ryan never really cared about doing that in public. So, I learned to just keep pace and walk along side of him. We walked over to the back side of the bar to the open patio where most of the party was taking place. We sat down at an empty little round table with high bar stools next to an old oak tree. The country music was loud and everyone was having a good time. It was a hot summer evening and the fresh country breeze felt so good against my face. I was happy that Ryan and I were finally doing something fun together.

A few minutes later he got up and headed over to the bar and returned with two ice cold bottles of beer. We quietly sipped on our cold beer listening to the music and watching happy couples tear up the dance floor. Ryan had always been very quiet around me, but when he was with his friends it was a different story. So, it didn't strike me strange that he would be quiet with me at the party. While I was sipping at my beer, I looked up at him and caught him staring at me. I didn't say anything to him because I thought that maybe he was just checking me out. I felt that it was an unusual stare, as if he wanted to tell me something but couldn't.

"Ryan, are you ok?" I asked.

He didn't answer me. Instead, he stood up, gulped down his beer and victoriously set the bottle down in front of me.

"We have to leave. I have something I need to do," he blurted.

My mouth dropped open as I looked up at him in disbelief. Surprised my chin didn't strike the table, I uttered, "Leave?" I couldn't believe he wanted to leave. We had only been there less than thirty minutes. I was enjoying my beer and was barely finished with it! I felt like a child in a grocery store following mom and whimpering because I couldn't get the candy that I wanted. I felt so foolish following him and almost begging him to stay. While approaching the truck, I tried to encourage him to stay so we could have a good time together. But my pleading and begging was non-existent in his ears. I remained quiet as he drove us back home. He pulled into the driveway and waited for me to get out of the truck. Without saying good-bye, he quickly backed out the truck leaving me nothing but a cloud of dust. I stood on the driveway watching him as he drove away. I was hoping he would come back, but he didn't.

One Saturday evening, Ryan and I had attended a big convention at a downtown fancy hotel. I remember holding onto his arm as we walked around the convention meeting and talking to our friends. Ryan was unusually quiet most of the time and had hardly said a word to me. I wasn't sure if he was bored or if he just had a lot on his mind. It was impossible to get him to open up and discuss any problems that he might be experiencing. I tried to be compassionate, because I knew the shooting incident that he was involved in still bothered him. So, I suggested that we go eat. Well, we left the convention center and headed over to a small Mexican restaurant located in the south side of town. We walked all the way to the back and sat down at a table near the kitchen. Ryan then started looking around the restaurant as if he were trying to avoid making eye contact with me.

"What's happening to us?" I wondered while stirring my coffee and watching the kitchen workers.

When I looked up, I caught him staring at me with that same serious tired look on his face. He was making me feel nervous.

"What's wrong?" I asked him.

He just shook his head and began eating his food quietly and slowly as if he were depressed. I couldn't enjoy my meal, I was concerned about his behavior.

"Is it the shooting incident?" I asked with concern.

"No!" he said shaking his head.

I knew that something was bothering him. But getting him to discuss his problems was impossible. I then gave up and reached over to pick up my cup of coffee when I noticed he was staring at me again. This time, his eyebrows were slightly raised.

"What is the matter? Is there something you want to tell me? Why are you acting so strange?" I asked with frustration in my voice.

He then stood up without saying a word and began walking toward the register to take care of the bill.

"Ok!" I said to myself pushing the plate away and getting up from my chair.

I felt embarrassed. I felt as if the whole restaurant knew that we were having problems. While driving home, I kept hoping the reason he was staring at me was because he thought I was beautiful, but it wasn't.

The Empty Dinner Chair

We lived in a big country house on twelve acres of land. The peace and quiet allowed me to hear the birds sing and the cows moo most of the day. The fresh country air and scenery always motivated me to find ways to make our home more comfortable, either by working in the yard, gardening, or baking. I enjoyed preparing delicious meals, especially making homemade tortillas from scratch and watching Ryan eat contently.

But lately, it seemed that almost every afternoon, he was not home on time for dinner. Ryan always showed up late, missing out on dinner with the excuse that he was helping out a friend, or because he was working at his dad's ranch. He refused to eat anything and would always head over to his office and shut the door. I never doubted his excuse because I knew he had rancher friends and that his father also was a rancher. I hoped he would return to the kitchen to check out what I had cooked and apologize for not being home for dinner, but he didn't.

There were times my husband would be sitting in the living room watching television and reading a magazine at the same time. I would call out to him a few times that dinner was ready, but he wouldn't respond. I never had to call the boys twice because they always showed up at the table hungry and ready to chow down. After calling Ryan several times, he finally would come and join us at the table. He would quickly serve his plate and wolf down his food.

Once he finished his meal, he would leave the table and head back to the living room without saying a word. I couldn't understand his strange quiet behavior at the table. The boys felt uncomfortable and were afraid to say a word. I tried my best to start conversations and make our dinner time together a little more enjoyable. After dinner, I slowly picked up the dinner dishes and started cleaning up. I was hoping Ryan would return to the kitchen and thank me for such a wonderful meal and ask for dessert like he would in the past, but he didn't.

The Couch Sleeping

I remember the first five years of our marriage were wonderful. Ryan and I would stay up late watching television. I always fizzed out and went to bed first. When Ryan would get tired he would turn off the TV and come to bed. I always felt so warm and secure when he would crawl under the sheets, putting his arm around my waist, holding me close to him. There were several times I would find him asleep on the couch and I would encourage him to come to bed. He would immediately get up from the couch still holding onto my hand while I led him to the bedroom. Well, it seemed like the last two years of our marriage he chose to make it a habit to sleep on the couch. Many times I would wake up in the night and find him asleep on the couch in a sitting position with the television still playing. Other times he would be sound asleep with an extra blanket he had removed from the children's bedroom. It was depressing to find him this way. I longed for him to come to bed and sleep with me like before, but he wouldn't.

Ryan enjoyed staying up late watching TV. Since I had to get up early for work the next day, I would kiss him good night and go to bed. Several hours into the night, I would wake up with the sound of the TV still blaring. I would get out of bed and check on him and sure enough, I would find him asleep on the couch. I never could figure out what was worse, trying to get a donkey to move or get your husband off the couch. Anyway, I would gently pull on his wrist trying to wake him up, while encouraging him to come to bed. I would whisper softly into his ear while rubbing his shoulder. After a few minutes and no response, I was getting a little frustrated. So, I started pulling his arm a little bit harder and speaking a little bit louder. Nothing worked. He would pull his arm back down, turn and lie on his side. I was beginning to hate that lousy couch. I would just give up and go back to bed. I would lie in bed looking at the ceiling feeling lonely and hurt. At times I would take my pillow and blanket and go into the living room and cuddle up on the floor next to the couch so I could be near him. When I would hear him move, I would just lie there very still watching him as he moved around trying to turn over on his side. I felt like a little puppy lying by the couch hoping my master would notice me. Once he was moving around on the couch when he suddenly stopped and propped himself up on his elbows. I could see that he was trying to focus his eyes on me. His silhouette looked scary in the dark. I wanted to laugh and kept tightening my lips.

"He must think I'm weird," I thought as I closed my eyes and held back from busting out laughing.

"Oh good, he notices me," I thought as I peeked at him over the edge of my blanket.

I then lowered the blanket from my face and looked up at him anxiously hoping he would wonder what I was doing on the floor. But instead he just turned over and went back to sleep. There were other times that I had attempted to snuggle next to him on the couch, which I discovered was impossible. I must have looked like a baby chick trying to crawl under mommy's wing. It was tough trying to lie next to him. We both didn't fit on the couch, and of course I always wound up sliding off onto the floor. I would jump back up on the couch and try it again. This time grabbing on to his arm so he could hold me next to him, but I couldn't even budge it out from under him. He didn't want me on the couch and he didn't care that I was on the floor. I remember standing next to the couch watching over him and wondering about his cold behavior.

"I don't think this man really loves me," I thought as I headed back to my lonesome bedroom. I was hoping he would come back to bed, but he didn't.

Starting Arguments

The first seven years of our marriage were wonderful until the last two years. It seemed I couldn't do anything right. Ryan would always find the most ridiculous reasons to start a fight. I was always the one who took charge of the bills and balanced the budget without any problem. One evening, I approached him while he was sitting up in bed reading. I went over and knelt by the bed and was going over the budget and explaining how much money we had left after paying the bills. He looked at me with an angry look on his face.

"You can't do anything right!" he scolded.

Of course being criticized this way for the first time caused me to become defensive. This started a small argument, which was enough for him to get up and leave the house. And I mean it was a small argument. We were not screaming or throwing things at each other, which is why it surprised me that he would just get up and leave. My feelings were hurt and I prayed that he would come back so that we could make up, but he didn't.

There were many other times that he would start fights just to give himself enough reason to leave the house. One afternoon we were all out in the driveway sitting in the truck getting ready to go visit my parents. Ryan was warming the truck, while I was in the process of separating forty dollars in my purse to give to my parents.

"What's the money for?" he asked.

While explaining to him that the money was for my parents, he quickly snatched the money from my hand and jumped out of the truck. I was shocked and couldn't believe what he had just done.

"What are you doing? Give me back that money!" I said laughingly. I jumped out of the truck and began chasing him around the front lawn. I knew we must have looked silly in front of the boys. They must have thought we were acting like children. He was running away from me waving the money up and down in the air like a little bully. I thought he was playing, but he was serious. He was not going to give me back that money. Then he pocketed the money and walked into the house. I was stunned! I began crying and couldn't believe that he would be so cruel. Ryan never had a problem lending money to anyone especially my parents, but why now? I was upset and felt so robbed. The visit to my parents was cancelled. A few minutes later he left in a hurry because he had something to do again. I was hoping he would stay home so we could try and makeup, but he didn't.

Scarce Phone Calls

Hello! Good-bye! I love you!… In the beginning of our marriage we always kept in touch by calling each other on the phone when we were apart. Ryan worked the night shift and was always out during the day helping out his friends or at his dad's ranch. During his regular shift at work he would call me at home and tell me that he loved me. Sometimes, he would even come home early just to surprise me. When he was down at Stanley's ranch helping with cattle, he would call me and let me know what he was doing and what time to expect him home. Toward the last year of our marriage his phone calls became fewer and fewer. And we had cellular phones. I was the one who had to initiate most of the phone calls just to keep in touch with him. Many times, I went to bed wondering where he was and why he hadn't called home. It finally got to a point where he wouldn't call home anymore. When I would ask him why he hadn't called me, he would get very defensive and use this as another reason to leave the house. Did he ever start calling me again? No, he didn't.

Sloppy Repairs

It was exciting when we moved into our new ranch house. I wanted everything to be perfect. So, I got busy hanging curtains, cleaning and getting everything in order. Ryan would head outside and cut the yard, fix the fences and take care of the minor repairs. He enjoyed cleaning the swimming pool and was always the first one to jump in, dragging me along with him. It was fun and I was glad that God had blessed us with so much. During the last year, I noticed that he was starting to lose interest in the house. He would ignore the outside chores and repairs. He just didn't care if the house was starting to look shabby.

The yard work and all other minor repairs became regular chores for me and the boys. It seemed all Ryan wanted to do when he was home was to sit and watch TV, read and fall asleep. Which I didn't mind at all. This was his castle and he could do whatever he wanted. Although, it would have been easier if he could just do his part instead of leaving it up to me to handle. The times that I did ask him to help me repair something, he would fix it rapidly with a bad attitude. There were times he would quit right in the middle of a project and leave the house, because of something important that he had to take care of. I already knew it would be hours before he returned, so I would finish the project myself. Many times I went to bed tired and hoping he would come home soon and appreciate me for finishing the repair, but he didn't.

I stood there on the deck looking at our one time clean swimming pool, which had turned into a green pond for bugs and frogs. So, I decided to stain the deck to improve its looks and have it ready for the summer, hoping this would spark Ryan's interest to clean the pool. I began spraying the deck carefully, board by board. After working for over an hour, I was getting pretty tired. I went into the house and found Ryan sitting on the couch watching television and talking to someone on the cellular phone.

"Ryan! Can you do me a favor? Can you finish spraying the deck so I can start dinner, please?" I asked.

He quickly turned off the cellular phone and walked outside and began spraying the deck, while I began preparing dinner. About ten minutes later, I went out onto the deck to see how he was doing. I went into instant shock to see that he not only sprayed the deck, but also the edges of the pool and the white limestone rock on the side of the house. I then shrieked to discover that he sprayed over and around the white lounging chairs missing the boards underneath them. I couldn't believe what my eyes were seeing, all of this covered in orange stain. When I commented about it, he threw down the sprayer.

"You don't appreciate anything!" he sarcastically answered.

He then went back into the house and quickly changed his clothes. He left again as usual stating that he had something to do. I then tried to get him to stay home and understand my reason for being upset. Did he stay? Did he understand? No, he didn't.

The Day Dreaming

What are you thinking about? That's what I used to ask him. Many times during the last year of our marriage, I would notice he would go into a trance. Sometimes, I would be talking to him about an incident that happened at work and he would just stare off into space. I used to think that maybe I was boring him, so I would quickly change the subject. If I asked him what he was thinking about, he would quickly answer, "nothing" and then leave the room. I tried to get him to talk out his problems, but he wouldn't.

I remember Christmas Eve, 1997, we were celebrating the holiday at my sister's house. I walked into the living room and found Ryan slumped on the couch staring at the wall. He was in a dream world of his own. It was frustrating because I never knew what he was thinking. I couldn't get him to express his feelings or discuss whatever it was that was bothering him. I never suspected that he was having an affair because he would constantly reassure me that he was not seeing another woman. But yet, he was constantly giving me the cold shoulder treatment. I felt lonely and hurt during this supposedly joyful time of the year. I yearned for him to hold me and tell me that nothing was wrong and that he loved me, but he didn't.

The Rejection

I walked into the bedroom with the laundry basket tucked under my arm. I was surprised to see Ryan all dressed up in his jeans and wearing a nice western shirt. Being curious, I asked him where he was going.

"I'm going to help out a friend," he said while putting on his boots.

"Why are you all dressed up?" I asked while following him as he made his way out the door and to his truck.

Of course I was following him. I was curious. He had been acting so suspicious lately and I was concerned over his strange behavior. He slowly climbed into his truck and looked at me through the driver window.

"Where are you going?" I asked again.

"I'll be right back," he assured me.

Knowing I wasn't going to get an answer. I decided to just kiss him good-bye. I walked up and stood behind the door. I placed my hand on his left thigh to give me a little support, so I could reach up and kiss him. Then he roughly pushed my hand off his thigh and turned his face away.

"What's wrong? Why are you acting this way?" I asked sounding surprised.

Ryan then placed his hand on my chest and pushed me away from the door and slammed it shut. He quickly backed his truck out of the driveway and left. While wiping the dust from my tearful eyes, I looked up to the sky through the tree branches and cried out to the Lord.

"Why God? Why is he rejecting me? What is going on with him?" I cried.

I could feel the hot tears flowing down my face as I turned and walked back into the house. I was hoping he would come back, but he didn't.

One evening, I stayed up late washing clothes, cleaning and taking care of other household chores so that I would be able to enjoy my day off on Saturday. It must have been at least 1:00 am when I decided to go to bed. Ryan had already been asleep for quite some time. I took a nice hot shower and applied soft scented lotion to my face and arms. I then brushed my long hair and quietly crawled under the warm sheets of our bed and snuggled up close to him. He was lying on his left side, so I placed my right arm over his waist and snuggled closer to him.

Suddenly, he turned around and with both hands he slowly pushed me far away toward the edge of my side of the bed nearly pushing me off. He then turned around and gave me his back. I didn't move. I couldn't move.

"What was that all about?" I thought as I laid there staring at his back.

"Why was he treating me this way? Is he rejecting me?" So many questions were running through my mind.

So, to verify, I reached over and gently touched his upper right arm, and sure enough, he quickly pulled away from me. Realizing that he was rejecting me, I silently cried to myself hoping he would regret what he was doing and turn around and hold me, but he didn't.

The Extra Clothing

He worked nights and I worked days. On his work nights, I would sit on the bed keeping him company while he got dressed for work. There were other times he would get dressed early without my knowledge and leave the house in a hurry. It was becoming a challenge just to get a good-bye kiss. More than several times while following behind him, I would notice him carrying extra clothes and a pair of tennis shoes under his arm.

"What's with the extra clothes?" I would ask curiously.

"I'm going to my dad's ranch in the morning to help out, is that ok with you?" he sarcastically answered. Trusting him, I accepted his answer in order to prevent an argument and watched him back up his truck and leave. I stood there again without a good-bye kiss and wondering why he had to help everyone out every morning. Was he telling me the truth? It was hard to tell. Sometimes, he really did go out to the ranch, but other times he didn't.

Dressing Different

Ryan was a macho man with a large mustache. He always dressed in western attire, boots and his favorite cowboy hat. During the last few months of our marriage, I noticed he started dressing different. He wasn't wearing his western shirts anymore. He started wearing a different style of shirt every time he came home.

"Why is he getting all these new clothes? He must be shopping on his own during the day while I'm at work," I thought.

This was strange, since we always shopped for clothes together. I thought that he looked nice and he had every right to wear what he wanted.

One afternoon, he came home while I was working on the budget. He walked right past me and picked up his mail. I sat still, curiously looking at him, because he was wearing a white polo shirt with cute little baseballs all over it. I didn't question him about his new look, because I didn't want to upset him. Once, he wore a plaid blue and green short sleeve shirt. It was very nice, although he reminded me of a little first grader wearing his new clothes for school. It didn't make any difference to me if he wore western or cute shirts. I loved him and he looked great in anything he wore. But for whatever reason, he was definitely acting strange. His quick arrivals and quick departures were driving me crazy. I kept refusing to believe that he might be seeing another woman. I was hoping he would stop leaving the house without saying good-bye, but he didn't.

His Laundry

Do clothes disappear on their own? I really don't think so. Many times my head would be stuck inside the laundry basket looking, flipping, and pulling clothes out searching for his under garments.

"Where are his tee shirts and underwear?" I would ask myself out loud.

During the first years of our marriage, I couldn't keep that laundry basket empty until the last year. That's when I began noticing that every time I washed the laundry, his clothes were becoming fewer and fewer. I thought that maybe he was leaving his laundry at the hunting cabin or at his father's ranch, since he was supposedly always over there working the cattle. If I questioned him about his laundry he would slowly walk away without answering me and act as if he didn't hear my question. Did he ever bring back his laundry? No, he didn't.

The Haircuts

Wow! You can cut hair? That's what Ryan first asked me when we met. Being a former hairdresser, I would cut Ryan's hair at least once a month. I always took my time to make sure his hair was cut right and looking great. He appreciated this because it saved him a trip to the shop and fourteen dollars. Toward the end of our marriage, I noticed his hair was looking slightly different. After several months of this, I began to wonder why he hadn't asked me to cut his hair.

"Ryan, where are you getting your hair cut?" I would ask him.

"Oh, I get it cut in town sometimes while running errands," he would answer me.

I remember one cold December afternoon, he came home and hurriedly began gathering up some of his things in the bedroom.

"Why are you in such a hurry?" I asked him.

"I have to help Stanley with his cattle," he quickly answered while heading toward the front door.

After noticing that his hair had grown out some, I encouraged him to stay so I could cut his hair. I purposely did this because I knew it would be my only chance to be near him and touch him, even if it was just his hair. So, I began cutting his hair while absorbing the feel of each soft strand between my fingers. I could tell that he was getting restless because he was in a hurry to get down to the ranch. I felt funny having to depend on cutting his hair just to feel close to him. It was enough to satisfy me since he had been rejecting me lately. Just touching his hair made my body tingle, because I loved him so much and I missed his closeness. In the past, while cutting his hair, he would interrupt my work by trying to tickle me or get fresh making me laugh. This time he sat there like an old sack of potatoes doing nothing but stare at the floor. While cutting near his left temple area, I slowly worked my way around until we were face to face. I tried to be slick and steal a kiss, but when I attempted, he turned his face and rejected me by asking me to hurry up the process. After I finished the haircut he quickly headed out the front door and jumped into his truck. I followed close behind him and stood inside the driver door looking at him as he started up the engine.

"Ryan, can I at least have a kiss before you go?" I asked.

He looked at me and nodded his head with consent and kissed me. Not just once, but three times.

"Do you still love me?" I asked.

"Yes," he said turning his face away.

"I love you too," I said before stepping away from the truck.

I stood back and watched him leave. He hadn't kissed me in weeks and I was hoping our kisses would stir up the silent love he had for me in his heart, but it didn't.

Separating Valuable Property

We bought a gun safe. In that safe we kept our duty weapons and all of Ryan's hunting rifles and shotguns. Ryan had an eye for handguns and was always bringing home another pistol or rifle to add to his collection. And having small children in the home, it was the best way to keep them out of their reach. One afternoon, I opened the gun safe and noticed that all the weapons were tagged with little white pieces of paper. As I read the tags it appeared that Ryan was separating the weapons by owners. Some were tagged with my father-in-law's name and one shotgun was tagged with my name.

"That's strange…why is he tagging all our weapons?" I asked myself while examining each tag.

The next day when I came home from work, I unlocked the gun safe and was surprised to discover that all the weapons were gone.

"Where are all the weapons? Where is my shotgun?" I asked myself out loud.

I stood there dazed with confusion staring into an empty gun safe.

"Is he…trying to leave me?" I wondered. Did he return the weapons? No he didn't.

The Excessive Drinking

Beer! Whiskey and more beer! It seemed he couldn't get enough. He drank at home, with his friends, after work and probably drank somewhere else too! Ryan was hardly ever home during the last few months of our marriage. Eating dinner alone with the boys every day was becoming a common thing for us. I was beginning to feel like a single parent all over again. When Ryan did come home he would head straight to the couch and drink some more. He would ignore my presence and refuse to carry a conversation with me. He would sit for hours drinking until he fell asleep. I remember one day, he was sitting on the couch sipping his beer and looking down at the floor.

"Ryan, what are you thinking about?" I asked softly with concern.

He didn't answer me, instead he quickly stood up and ran down the hallway and out the front door.

"Ryan! Where are you going?" I pleaded as I followed after him.

He was too fast for me and I couldn't catch up to him. By the time I made it outside, he had already gotten into his truck and started up the engine. We both looked into each other's eyes as he backed the truck out of the driveway. I stood near the driveway feeling confused and abandoned as I watched the truck disappear down the road. Well, he was gone and he didn't come home all night. The next morning, I jumped out of bed and ran to the couch hoping I would find him there. The couch was empty and not a single pillow was disturbed. This was one time, I found myself wishing he were asleep on the couch.

"He's not here!" I whispered to myself as I began frantically searching the house. He was not home. *"Where is he? Is he cheating on me? Is he? Is he?"* I kept asking myself.

Later that afternoon, I realized that worrying was not going to get me anywhere. I felt sorry for the boys because they knew that I was sad. So, I decided to take them out for ice cream.

"Come on boys. Let's walk down to the corner dime store for ice cream!" I called out.

Once we walked into the store, the boys ran off to the ice cream freezer, while I headed over to the register.

"Hi there!" yelled Mr. Davis from the back of the store.

"Hello Mr. Davis!" I yelled back.

"Hey, what was wrong with Ryan last night?" he asked.

"I don't know. He left the house and didn't come home all night," I answered quietly so the boys wouldn't hear me.

"Why? Do you know something?" I asked.

"I don't know what was bothering him last night. He stayed drinking outside until closing time, got really drunk and took off. I thought he was heading back out toward your place," he explained.

"No, he didn't come home," I answered sadly while paying for the ice cream.

"Well, you let me know if you and the boys need anything. I'd be glad to help," he offered.

"Thank you," I answered.

So, he drank until closing time and failed to come home. Where did he go? Did he come home that day? No, he didn't

Loss of Interest

It was Christmas morning 1997, and I was awakened by the sound of excited little voices coming from the living room. The boys were already up and tearing open their Christmas gifts.

"Ryan, it's Christmas morning. The kids are up and opening their gifts," I said gently waking him up.

"Here dad this one is for you!" yelled little Tyler eagerly handing him a gift as we entered into the living room. Ryan expressed no emotions at all. Instead, he just sat quietly on the couch with nothing but an old frown on his face, while Tyler piled the gifts on his lap. He quietly watched the boys as they tore open their gifts, while ignoring me at the same time. He wouldn't even crack a smile. As much as he was ignoring me and not participating with the boys, I still felt compassion for him. I knew he was unhappy and that he was suffering from something that he didn't want to talk about. I wanted so much for him to talk to me and share whatever it was that was bothering him.

I stood up and walked over to the couch where he was sitting and slowly knelt down on the carpet next to him. He didn't even acknowledge my presence and remained quiet. I noticed the stone cold look on his face as he watched the boys unwrap their gifts. I could tell that he was purposely ignoring me. He wouldn't even look at me. "Merry Christmas," I whispered as I reached over his lap and picked up one of his gifts.

"Here, open your gift," I said softly.

He took the gift from my hand and carelessly placed it on his lap allowing it to slide off and fall onto the floor. *"That's it!"* I thought. Something was terribly wrong with him and I was beginning to lose my patience.

"Ryan, please talk to me. Why are you acting this way?" I asked. He turned and gave me one hard look and then quickly piled the gifts on the couch. He stood up and headed toward our bedroom. I followed behind him. He opened the closet door and began searching through his shirts. I watched curiously as he selected a light blue western shirt. He then removed the hanger and threw it on the bed. With the shirt clutched in his hand, he then walked out of the bedroom and headed straight toward the laundry room.

"What in the world is he doing?" I thought.

I followed behind him into the laundry room, not realizing that I was about to see something I had never seen before. Ryan unfolded the ironing board, plugged in the iron and began ironing his shirt. I couldn't believe what my eyes were seeing. Now, I was really convinced that Ryan was being strange. In the nine years of our marriage he never ironed his clothes, so it struck me strange to observe this.

"Ryan! What are you doing? Why are you ironing this shirt?" I curiously asked.

"I'm leaving you!" he said coldly.

I felt the blood drain from my face as the words rang in my ears. My heart sank and I felt instantly nauseous.

"What did you say?"

"I said, I'm leaving you!"

"Why?" I asked frantically.

The tears quickly began forming in my eyes. I couldn't believe what he was saying. I began pleading with him hoping he would change his mind. I wanted him to hold me and tell me that he was just kidding.

"Why? What have I done?" I cried.

"It's nothing you've done?" he answered bluntly.

"Then why are you doing this? Is it another woman?" I asked starting to cry.

Ryan wouldn't answer me anymore. The more I cried and begged, the more he ignored me. I remember falling down to my knees next to the ironing board. I was crying and pleading with him for forgiveness.

"Please forgive me for whatever I have done, please forgive me, just like Jesus forgives us, please!" I begged with broken sobs.

"It's nothing you've done!" he insisted while putting on his shirt. He then walked around me and out of the laundry room. I quickly got up from my knees and followed behind him still crying. I was sick with hurt from the shocking news, and embarrassed to see my children standing in the dining room with curious looks on their faces. My two daughters were visiting for Christmas and surely were not expecting something like this.

"What are you doing to mom!" yelled my eldest daughter Sarah.

"I'm leaving your mother!" he yelled back while heading toward the front door.

I was frantic and the kids were shocked. I followed Ryan outside pleading with him not to leave me and the kids. Once he was out the front door, he ran towards his truck as fast as he could with me still following behind him. He jumped into his truck and pushed me away before slamming the truck door shut.

"Is it another woman?" I asked with desperation.

"No!" he yelled from the open window.

"Please don't leave me, don't do this to us, I love you," I cried.

It was a cold Christmas morning and the chilling breeze was cutting through my nightgown. I clung onto the truck's open window shaking and crying. I pleaded for him not to leave me while he yanked my fingers off the door frame. He then backed up the truck as fast as he could and left me standing again in the middle of another dust cloud. "No, God! This can't be happening. Why God? Why?" I asked tearfully, while looking up into the sky.

I stayed outside for a while shaking and crying in the cold breeze. The hot tears kept pouring out of my eyes as I clung onto the old oak tree by the driveway. I tried to focus through blurred vision on the distant roadway hoping he would change his mind and come back. Ice cold breezes came in separate intervals cutting through my chest and face. I was cold and my body began to shake uncontrollably. I didn't care if I froze to death. At that very moment, I wanted to die. The ferocious pain in my heart was so unbearable that even death seemed soothing. The man I loved was gone. Our future, our dreams and all our hopes destroyed, and I still didn't know why. After what seemed like hours, I ran back into the house. The kids were quiet and had angry looks on their faces, except for little Tyler who sat low in his chair at the dinner table almost hiding his face.

"It's ok mom, let him go, he's not worth it, he probably has another woman," said Sarah.

"No, don't say that!" I cried.

"Well, why else do you think he is leaving?"

"I don't know, but he has been acting strange lately."

"He probably has another woman, you don't need him mom," she said doing her best to comfort me.

I felt exhausted from so much crying. My body was completely numb and tremendously weak. The pain in my heart was unbelievable.

"This can't be happening," I thought repeatedly. I wanted this nightmare to end. I wanted my Ryan to come back, but he didn't.

The New Vehicle

Ok, my husband left us Christmas morning 1997. Where did he go? Nobody knew. Not even one of his co-workers knew anything, or at least they weren't saying. Two weeks later, I was shocked to see Ryan walk into my work place. He walked up to my workstation and just stood there looking down at me. I sat pinned in my chair staring up at him. I was speechless. I couldn't believe he was standing before me. I felt weak, hurt and angry all at the same time. I was still suffering from the deep wounds I experienced on Christmas morning and my feelings were confused for a split second. I didn't know whether to hug him or walk away from him. I didn't know if I was mad or glad. As I looked around the room, I noticed that my co-workers were trying their best not to stare. They all knew that Ryan had walked out on me on Christmas morning, because they all did their best to comfort me during that difficult time.

I got up from my chair and walked into the break room. I kept my back toward the door to prevent from seeing him because I knew he had followed me. I heard him as he walked into the room. I could feel his presence close behind me. I was nervous and afraid of what he might say to me. I stood there slightly shaking with my eyes closed. I didn't want to turn around. I didn't want to look at him.

"I need you to co-sign for a new truck that I want to buy," he explained.

My eyes quickly popped opened and the shaking stopped. I could feel the tension and anger rising from within me. I then tightened my eyes to fight back the tears that were trying to force their way out. I couldn't believe what he was asking me. I quickly turned myself around and walked up to him. I was no longer afraid to see his face. I put my face so close to his that our noses almost touched.

"I can't believe you left me and the kids and all you can think about is buying a stupid truck," I whispered clenching my teeth.

He was so desperate in wanting to buy a new truck that he almost began begging me to help him buy it. After several attempts in trying to convince me to co-sign, he finally realized that he wasn't going to get my cooperation and furiously stormed out of the break room.

"I'm divorcing you," he angrily threatened while pointing his finger in my direction.

Well, I'll say that was some great entertainment for my co-workers. So, was he buying the new truck for us to enjoy? No, he wasn't.

Your Intuition

One of God's most beautiful gifts to women is the gift of intuition. During this whole ordeal my intuition kicked in many times trying to warn me that my husband was having an affair. That's right! My own God given intuition. I don't know why I ignored it so many times. I guess I loved my husband so much that I just couldn't bring myself to believe that he might be involved with another woman. It just seemed easier to convince myself day and night that the shooting incident had something to do with his behavior.

"Is he?" That nagging little question seemed to nip at me constantly trying to get my attention. And many times, I would extinguish it and go about my business. I should have listened to my intuition, but I didn't.

I Trusted

I trusted the rain to cleanse me
I trusted the wind to strengthen my course
I trusted the sun to entice me

When the rain came, I learned
When the winds howled, I held on for dear life
When the sun's rays kissed my face, I rejoiced

The sun would shine its wondrous light
Providing warmth to our heart's delight
It helped me grow and kept us warm at night
But clipped my eye and lost his sight

The wind would blow and change directions
To and fro, its own discretion
I was to, and he was fro
I would stay, and he would go

The rain then came and washed away the
bridge of hope, alone I stood that day

The waters rose and left us asunder
I cried to the heavens, he sought her thunder
I fought for love, lust filled his eye
My dreams were shattered, he didn't say good-
bye

Aileen Christine

Holding on to things I trusted
Left me alone and emotionally busted
They say true-love belong together
Truth be told, only One Love lasts forever

The Way, the Truth and the Life
"I do," I will stand with others and be His wife

In Him I trust alone persevering and rejoicing
till the day I go home.

Gary J. Silva, Poem writer

Chapter 1

It was a cold night in middle December. I woke up terrified from a frightening nightmare. I was afraid and quickly got out of bed and checked on Ryan and the boys. Ryan was sound asleep on the couch and the boys were in their rooms sleeping peacefully. Although Ryan had been rejecting me lately, I still felt safe and secure knowing that he was home. I wanted to be near him, so I sat on the couch next to him and thought about the vicious nightmare that I had dreamt earlier.

"What kind of nightmare was that?" I asked myself.

I dreamt I was sitting inside the sanctuary of a large church when a dark haired woman came and sat next to me. We didn't speak and the woman glanced at me with a strange look in her eyes. Then she got up and walked out of the sanctuary and down the hall. I felt compelled to follow her. As I was walking down the hallway, I saw the dark haired woman struggling with a man on the floor.

I looked at myself and I was surprised to see that my clothes had transformed into a full police uniform. I quickly responded to the woman's aid and attempted to pull the man away from her. The man was resisting and ignoring my verbal commands to stop. The man and woman continued to viciously scuffle on the floor.

With one last attempt, I forcefully managed to place the man's arms behind his back and handcuff him. I escorted him to a nearby chair and sat him down. The woman then disappears. Suddenly, I was speaking to another police officer who had arrived at the scene to back-me-up. As I was briefing him on the situation, the man began to laugh in a deep raspy devilish tone of voice. "Ha! Ha! Ha!" laughed the man. I could feel the chill of terror run its way up my spine as I slowly turned to look at the man. He was looking at me with a wicked grin on his face and his eyes were bloodshot red.   He was holding the handcuffs in his right hand, swinging them back and forth victoriously. I stood by watching as my partner quickly struggled with the man and held him down on the floor. I watched as my partner pulled out a pistol grip drill and began fastening the man's right hand to the floor. The blood was spurting from his hand as the screw made its way through. I cupped my hands over my mouth as I watched the man yell in agony as his hand was being drilled. He was yelling and frantically moving his head from left to right. He then looked at me with blood soaked eyes and I felt tremendous compassion for him. Then suddenly a kind man with his hands cuffed in front walked past me and sat down on the same chair. The kind man had long brown shoulder length hair and wore a white shirt and a light brown corduroy blazer. He was so gentle. His face expressed nothing but love and kindness as he looked at me. The sounds of agony coming from the other man faded away as I focused on the kind man.

Two weeks after that dreadful nightmare, Ryan left us on Christmas morning. I wasn't sure if the dream had any significance in Ryan's leaving or the trial that was yet to befall me, but soon I was about to find out. I prayed constantly asking God to forgive me for being a bad wife. I prayed wholeheartedly pledging to God that I would be the submissive wife that I needed to be, if Ryan came back to me.

It was early January when I was transferred to the Personal Recognizance Department at the courthouse, where I processed persons with active warrants. One morning I had just walked into the office when I received a phone call at my desk.

"PR Bonds, this is Officer Stinson. Can I help you?" I answered.

"Hello? It's me, Ryan," the voice on the other end said. I was surprised to hear his voice and held my breath for a quick second.

"Ryan?" I asked in wonderment.

"Look Aileen, I know last week you refused to co-sign for that truck I've been wanting to buy. But you must remember that you are still my wife and I need your help. I really need to buy this truck and I can't do it without your signature. Will you please help me?" he pleaded kindly.

My heart melted. It felt so good to hear his voice again and I wanted to see him. A quick flashback of my recent prayer reminded me of trying to be the submissive wife that I needed to be. Not wanting to be a hypocrite in God's eyes, I went ahead and agreed to co-sign for him.

"Ok, I'll do it," I said.

"You will?" he asked sounding relieved.

"Yes, I'll do it because I love you," I told him.

"Ok, then I will be right down with the paperwork for you to sign," he said.

"No! Not here. Not at my workplace. Let's meet at the taco restaurant on the corner at eight thirty and I will sign the paperwork there," I instructed.

I looked up at the clock and it read eight fifteen and I was getting anxious about meeting with Ryan. I stepped out of the building and stood at the top of the steps of the courthouse. I wanted to allow myself a few minutes to pray for guidance before our meeting. As I silently prayed, I could hear a woman singing in the distance. Her voice was soft and harmonious. I looked around and focused my attention on a dark skinned woman who was walking up the sidewalk. She was wearing a long white garment trimmed with gold ribbon around the edges. The garment was draped neatly around her body. She wore on her head a white turban decorated with gold trim and colorful rhinestones. There was something definitely different about her. I watched her as she sang angelically to herself as she walked up the sidewalk. She stopped at the foot of the steps and looked up at me.

"Child! I can see trouble in your face!" she said loudly.

I wasn't sure if she was speaking to me. I looked around and didn't see anyone in the area. I didn't answer her just in case I was wrong and didn't want to embarrass myself. I watched her with amusement as she continued singing while ascending the steps. When she made it to the top of the steps, she walked directly toward me and looked me straight in the eye. She was beautiful. There was a brilliance shining from her face and her features were so delicate.

"I see trouble in your face. What is bothering you child?" she asked kindly.

"My husband left me several weeks ago and now he wants me to co-sign some…," before I could finish explaining, she quickly interrupted me.

"No! Don't sign any papers! Child don't do it!" she insisted excitedly.

The woman then placed her hand on my forehead and began praying; *"Dear Father in heaven, we come before you and plead your mercy upon us. Bless this child and give her the wisdom to make the right decisions. We pray that the Holy Spirit will guide her and lead her during this most difficult time in her life. We thank you and praise you almighty God. In Jesus name, Amen."*

"Now remember, whatever you do, always listen to the Holy Spirit. If your spirit is disturbed when you get ready to sign those papers, then don't do it. If you feel peace within your heart then it is ok," she said instructing me before stepping away.

I thanked her and then looked at my watch and it read eight twenty nine. I turned to look back at the woman and she was gone. I looked through the glass entrance doors and could not catch a glimpse of her anywhere in the hallway. Well, I surely wasn't expecting something like that this morning, but I was thankful anyway. I hurried down the steps and ran across the street and into the restaurant. I saw Ryan sitting toward the back at a large table. He already had the paperwork spread through out the table. I pulled out a chair and sat down next to him. Instead of him acknowledging my presence, he quickly began pointing to the dotted lines on each page where my signature was needed. I picked up the pen. Ryan then began shoving the paperwork in front of me for my signature. As soon as I placed the tip of the pen on the dotted line, I immediately felt a flutter inside the middle of my chest. I quickly looked up at Ryan remembering what the dark skinned woman had warned me.

"If your spirit is disturbed when you get ready to sign those papers, don't do it," I recalled her saying.

"Ryan? If I sign these papers will you come back home to us?" I asked carefully.

I could see the anger building up in his eyes as he aggressively looked back at me.

"Sign here, and here, and here, and here," he instructed pointing quickly to the different pages.

The fluttering became intense and my spirit was highly convicted. I couldn't sign those papers, so I laid the pen back down on the table. Ryan knew what my actions meant and he angrily gathered up the paperwork and stood up looking at me with hate in his eyes.

"I'm divorcing your ass!" he threatened before walking away from the table.

I sat still. My heart felt as if it were bleeding. There were a few people in the restaurant and I knew they had heard him. I was hurt and felt embarrassed. A few minutes later, I headed back to my office thinking about the woman and her advise. I gave thanks to God and began praying and hoping that Ryan didn't mean what he said about divorcing me.

It was February. The weeks were flying by and I still didn't know why Ryan had left us on Christmas morning. I hadn't seen or heard from him, except for the two times he attempted to get me to co-sign for that truck he wanted so badly. It was almost as if he had disappeared from the world. Everyday, I would call family members, our friends and his co-workers and no one seemed to know his whereabouts. The thought of Ryan never coming back and losing him forever haunted my mind. I would wake up every night and cry out uncontrollably, pleading with God to bring him back home. I would lie in bed for hours thinking about how I was going to manage the ranch and take care of the boys on a single salary. I felt so small as I thought about the twelve acres of land, the ranch house and the bills, as well as the kids. Why would Ryan leave and abandon me with so much responsibility to bear alone. The fear of having to survive on my own without Ryan was frightening and I would grieve until I fell asleep. Once, I woke up in the middle of the night stretching my arms up toward the ceiling. I wanted God to take my hands and pull me up into the heavens with Him, rescuing me out of this miserable nightmare. My heart and spirit were crushed and the pain was unbearable. By the time morning came, I felt exhausted from so much crying that I would find myself calling work and explaining that I was too sick to report for duty. Every morning, I would get out of bed and check every room in the house to see if Ryan had come home during the night. His office was exactly the same as he had left it that dreadful morning. It was not until Ryan left me that I began trusting in God for answers. I should have first turned to God when my intuition kicked in, but instead, I chose to ignore it and God, hoping Ryan would change with time.

One morning, while I sat in my truck warming the engine, I looked around the twelve acres and noticed how beautiful everything looked against the early morning sunrise. The butterflies were busily touching down on the roses and the birds were perched along the fence line chirping. The grassy fields showed off their rich green and yellow colors as they swayed back and forth dancing with the wind. The sweet country smell filled the air as the cool morning breeze blew through the truck's open windows. Although it was refreshing, I still felt sad and so alone.

"How could he leave me and all what God had blessed us with?" I wondered.

I began praying and thanking God for everything that He had given us. I looked up into the heavens searching for God's face and began praying out loud,

"Father, I don't know where Ryan is. Can you please reveal his whereabouts? I love him and I need to know what is going on. Please help me find him. Thank you."

I then backed out of the driveway and drove off to work. It was only a couple of hours into the shift when Officer Tim Perry walked into the office.

"Hi Aileen," he greeted with a big smile.

"Hey Tim, how are you doing?" I asked.

"I'm doing just fine, how about yourself?" he asked with concern.

"Oh, I'm hanging in there, just taking it one day at a time," I replied while sorting through paperwork.

"Say, you know what? I may be wrong, but this morning, I could've sworn I saw Ryan driving his truck out of the Meadow Hills Apartments," he said.

I immediately stopped what I was doing and looked up at Officer Perry.

"You saw him? I haven't seen him since he left me Christmas morning, except for the two times he came around begging me to co-sign for a new truck," I explained.

"Well, it looked like he was driving a brand spanking new truck," he said. "Yea, I heard he convinced his parents to co-sign for that truck. Are you sure it was him?" I asked.

"Yea, I'm pretty sure it was him. But of course I could be wrong. Well, I have to go now but if you need anything just let me know," he said while walking back out into the hallway.

"Thanks Tim. Thanks for telling me," I yelled back.

"So, that's where he's been staying," I thought to myself. I stood up from my desk, closed my eyes and began thanking God. *"Thank you God for hearing my prayer this morning. Thank you for revealing his whereabouts,"* I whispered.

I then walked out of the office and headed over to the 127th District Court to get the judge's approval on some bond releases. As I walked into the court

77

room, I saw old Judge James Darwin sitting at the bench by himself immersed in a huge law book. Judge Darwin must have been at least eighty five years old. He had been a judge for over forty five years and had heard almost every case imaginable.

"Hi Judge Darwin," I greeted.

"Hello Officer Stinson," he answered softly.

I walked up behind the bench and stood on the second step and handed him the paperwork.

"I just need your approval on these bonds judge," I said. "Sure, no problem," he answered.

He was so friendly and always took the time to speak to anyone who came before him. I felt like a little girl standing next to him as I watched him scribble his name across the sheets of paper. Judge Darwin had a grandfather figure about him and he always made me feel comfortable around him.

"Judge? Can I ask you something?"

"Sure, what's on your mind?"

"My husband left me on Christmas morning and I found out that he might be staying at some apartments near town. You know judge, several years ago, he killed a man while in the line of duty. I know he was having a hard time dealing with it. Do you think that's the reason why he left me?" I asked.

"No, he left you for another woman," he answered bluntly. I blinked several times stunned by his blatant answer.

"What?" I asked with disbelief.

"Oh, yea! It's always another woman. Why else would he leave you," he assured me.

I wanted to cry and couldn't bear to hear what else Judge Darwin had to say. My throat felt hard and cold as I fought back the tears. Judge Darwin kept speaking, but his words were faint and distant as the possibility of another woman swirled through my mind.

"I have to go now judge, I have a lot of work I need to catch up on," I answered as I walked out of the courtroom. Judge Darwin knew that I was hurting and it was not his fault. I asked a question and got an answer I didn't want to hear.

"I'm sorry I had to tell you like that. But, that's always the case in those types of situations," he explained while sticking his head back into the huge law book.

I stopped and turned to look at Judge Darwin over my right shoulder. I was angry toward him for afflicting my spirit with his honest opinion.

"No, judge! Ryan wouldn't do that to me. I think he just needs some type of counseling," I explained while exiting the courtroom. I felt angry and embarrassed. I didn't want the judge or anyone else to think that I got dumped for another woman. I refused to except the judge's answer, although it did linger in my mind continuously.

"Did he?" Did he really leave me for another woman? Can Judge Darwin be right?" I thought.

As I was walking down the main hallway, I was dispatched to the north entrance doors to check on someone who possibly was carrying a weapon. Upon arriving, the security guard informed me that the gentleman standing near the x-ray machine had a handgun in his briefcase. I then looked at the x-ray machine's monitor and saw the image of a handgun. I opened the briefcase and saw in plain view a .357 cal. handgun. After further investigation, I then advised the gentleman that he was under arrest for unlawfully carrying a weapon. The gentleman then nervously laughed and introduced himself as Attorney Noel Fazio. Mr. Fazio was very well known for his million dollar law firm. I then placed Mr. Fazio under arrest and escorted him to the holding cell for further processing. Later that afternoon, Mr. Fazio was released on a PR Bond. From that day forward Mr. Fazio always made it a point to greet me or stop by my desk and carry a conversation with me. He had a very good sense of humor and I almost felt bad arresting him.

Chapter 2

That afternoon, after work, I drove straight to the Meadow Hills apartments to search for Ryan. Once I arrived, I slowly pulled into the main entrance driveway and parked my car along side the curb. I sat in the car for awhile studying the large apartment complex which was divided into three separate buildings. Searching for Ryan would be like looking for a needle in a haystack. So, I decided to just drive around the parking area hoping to catch sight of him standing outside near one of the apartments. As I drove around, I couldn't believe the many cars and trucks that were parked. I wasn't sure what Ryan's truck looked like, except that it was dark blue in color. I stopped my truck to examine my surroundings and began praying silently.

"Oh my God, I need your help again. There are so many trucks parked out here. How will I know which one is Ryan's. Please help me find him Lord. Only you know where he is. Please help me find him," I prayed.

Feeling overwhelmed, I started up the engine and began driving up and down the rows of cars and trucks hoping to find a clue. I began feeling a little anxious as I drove through the last building's parking lot. When I drove around the corner of the building, I noticed a shiny dark blue, double cab, four wheel drive, parked all alone in a row of empty parking spaces. Somehow, deep down inside me, I knew it had to be Ryan's truck, but I had to make sure. So, I quickly jotted down the license plate number and headed back home. The next morning at work, I ran the license plate number through our dispatch office and it came back registered to a "Ryan Albert Stinson." My heart sank with pain as I leaned back into my chair.

"Why is he staying there? Why would he leave me and get an apartment? Was I that bad of a wife that he would leave me and the kids?" I thought to myself.

It was hard getting through the rest of the day at work and it seemed like the clock was purposely taking its time. My co-workers knew something was wrong and dared not to ask. I sat at my desk in deep thought wondering why Ryan had left me. So, I decided that the next day, Saturday morning I would go back to the apartment complex and search for him once again. This time hoping to find him and convince him to come back home.

Early that Saturday morning, I drove back out to the apartment complex. I parked the truck and walked straight to the manager's office. The door bell sounded off several times as I walked through the door alerting the elderly receptionist standing behind the desk. She peered at me through her small framed glasses.

"Can I help you?" she asked.

"Yes ma'am. Can you please tell me if you have a Ryan Stinson staying in these apartments?"

After what seemed like hours, she casually looked up at me from behind the computer screen.

"Nope, no one here by that name," she said.

"Are you sure?" I asked.

"Yes, I'm sure. There is no Ryan Stinson checked into these apartments. He just might be staying with a friend," she explained.

"Ok, well thanks for your help," I said walking out of the office.

I sat in my car for a few minutes thinking about what I needed to do next. *"Ok, so he's not renting an apartment. Maybe the receptionist is right, he might be staying with one of his buddies, but which one and where?"* I thought. I then drove toward the last building and parked my car next to Ryan's truck. After allowing myself a few minutes to build up enough courage, I exited my car and began knocking on apartment doors hoping to find him. I must have knocked on at least thirty or forty doors with no luck and I was starting to get tired. The thought of giving up and going home crossed my mind, but I didn't care. I loved Ryan and I was determined to find my man and bring him home. While ascending the stairwell to apartment #120C, I noticed the front door was wide open and I was able to see into the living room through the screen door. I knocked once and after waiting a couple of seconds, I noticed a skinny woman peeking at me from around the kitchen door. She had long dark hair parted down the middle, high arched eyebrows and sunken cheeks. The woman then cautiously walked up to the screen door staring at me with a questionable look on her face.

"Hello, I am looking for a man named Ryan Stinson. Would you happen to know where he might be staying?" I asked her.

Instead of her answering me, she quickly locked the latch on the screen door and began slowly walking backwards down the narrow hallway. Her fiery eyes were fixed upon me as she viciously knocked on one of the bedroom doors. I watched with curiosity as she spoke to someone through the bedroom door. I thought that maybe she didn't speak English and that she was trying to get someone to come out and speak with me. Suddenly, a man wearing a white tee shirt and blue jeans steps out into the hallway. It was Ryan! I could feel the pulsation of my heart beating faster and harder as I watched them whisper amongst themselves. My face was pressed against the screen as I watched them in suspense.

"Ryan!" I desperately called out.

He came and stood behind the screen door with his arms crossed against his chest. He gazed at me at close range through the screen without saying a word. There was a hardness about his face and he appeared angry. I noticed his once beautiful green eyes had lost their sparkle and were now dull and emotionless. I was terribly nervous and confused with his harsh appearance and intimidating stance. Before I could speak a word, the woman casually walked up next to him and cupped her hands around his upper left arm, as if she were claiming her property. A quick flashback of Judge Darwin's words flashed across my mind.

"He's left you for another woman!" I remembered him saying.

Although, the hard cold evidence was standing directly in front of me, I still ignored the fact that Ryan had left me for another woman. I don't remember feeling anything at the moment, all I knew was that I had found Ryan and I needed to convince him to come back home.

"Ryan, what are you doing? Why are you here and who is this woman?" I questioned.

Before Ryan could answer, the woman suddenly began screaming in a high pitched tone of voice,

"You need to get the hell off of my property!" she yelled.

I continued ignoring her demands and blocking out her vulgarities as I tried to focus on Ryan. He was acting so strange, as if he were under a spell of some sort. He was silent and unresponsive to my questions. There was something different about him. He was definitely not the same man I once knew.

"Ryan, what has happened to you? Say something!" I whispered pleadingly through the screen.

I was looking directly into his eyes. I wanted so desperately to get through to him and snap him out of his entrancement. It appeared that he was bewitched. His eyes were stagnant as he quietly stared at me through the screen door.

"I told you to get the hell off of my property, or I will call security!" the woman threatened yelling through the top of her voice.

This time she really upset me. I had enough of her interruptions. This was my husband and I was not going to let her destroy my marriage and steal my husband from me. I quickly looked at her and calmly pointed my finger in her direction,

"I rebuke you Satan! In Jesus name, now get back!" I commanded, not speaking directly toward her, but to the enemy behind the scenes of destruction and affliction. Quietly and obediently the woman stepped away from Ryan and headed back into the kitchen.

"Amen! There is power in the name of Jesus," I quickly thought to myself as I looked back at Ryan.

"Ryan! Please snap out of it! I'm your wife and we have a son. Please Ryan say something," I pleaded.

I was totally alarmed at his unresponsiveness. He seemed so brainwashed. His eyes were so distant as if he were hypnotized and I was afraid for him.

"Why don't you get the hell out of here and leave us alone!" the woman yelled while clinging onto his arm again.

Her voice rumbled in my ears as I noticed her villainous eyes piercing at me through stringy strands of hair. I stood back and looked at both of them. I felt remarkably confident that the angels of God were standing behind me, supporting me.

"This is my husband! What you two are doing is adultery. If you both don't stop, God's punishment can come upon you," I warned them.

"Why don't you get your Jesus and get the hell out of here!" the woman bellowed.

I quickly looked at Ryan and saw him drop his head downward. I knew he was affected by the woman's evil comment. Somehow, it managed to break him out of his trance temporarily. My spirit was offended by her comment and I felt afraid for both of them. I gave Ryan one last look and then ran down the stairwell back to my truck.

"Judge Darwin was right all along. Ryan did leave me for another woman. But why would he leave his family and all what he had for such a callous woman like that," I wondered with tears streaming down my cheeks.

As the minutes ticked by, the obsession in wanting my husband back grew stronger and stronger each minute. I wanted my husband back and I was not going to give up the fight so easily.

Chapter 3

I sat at the kitchen table sorting through family photos. I had bought a large photo album and started arranging photos beginning with our marriage, the birth of our son, family members, the ranch house, cattle and all the happy events we shared together during our marriage. The object of the game was to try and spark back the memories in Ryan's mind, hoping he would realize what a mistake he was making and come back home to us. On the last page of the album, I inserted a pink heart shaped piece of paper with the words; "We love you, please come home." I spent hours putting the album together and it was tiresome. Feeling weary, I rested my head on the table and thought about Ryan coming home and back into my arms again. I would have forgiven him in a second. I then ran my fingers across the top of the album and cried until I fell asleep.

The next afternoon, I drove back to the apartment complex and parked next to Ryan's truck. I got out of my truck with the photo album tucked under my arm. I quickly scanned the area to make sure it was clear and then I ran and placed the album inside the bed of his truck. While driving back home, I thought about Ryan and his affair. I felt embarrassed and ashamed for what he was doing. Many times, I had found myself comforting my co-workers and friends when their marriages fell apart, while at the same time feeling fortunate that I had a wonderful marriage.

Ryan and I had been married for nine years and everyone knew us. We were the Stinsons and we were very well respected. How little did I know that one day, I would find myself in the same situation as my co-workers and friends. A few days later, I began calling family members and informing them that Ryan was living with another woman. As soon as they would answer the phone, I would start grieving tearfully as I tried to explain the tragic news to them. Some family members were angry and advised me to let him go while others prayed for God to help save the marriage. I would stay in my room and cry for hours, praying late into the night that Ryan would leave the other woman and come back home. Two weeks had gone by since I discovered Ryan's affair and still he hadn't called or even come by to check up on his mail. I had cried so much that my lower eyelids and cheeks were starting to get chapped from the many tears that were being shed.

Every afternoon after dinner, the boys would run around and play, while I sat on the porch steps waiting and hoping for Ryan's truck to pull around from the long stretched road. I wouldn't leave until after the sun had set and the darkness came. I would go back into the house and lock the front door feeling disappointed. Another day had gone by and Ryan still hadn't come home. Although the boys were home, I still felt alone.

Every night after the boys had fallen asleep, I would take my bible and go into my bedroom closet, turn on the light and shut the door. I would place a black lace prayer veil on my head, shut my eyes and begin praying. The closet became my confessional where I cried and expressed myself to God. I wanted to be apart from the rest of the world that was so full of adultery and wickedness of all sorts. I found more serenity in the closet talking to God then anywhere else I've ever known.

One day, I neatly placed a setting on the dining table where Ryan usually sat for dinner. A plate, bowl, drinking glass, knife, fork and a spoon. The boys were instructed not to touch the setting because dad was still the head of the household and was expected to return soon. A few weeks later, Tyler approached me in the kitchen while I was washing dishes.

"Mom, when is dad coming home? His plate is already getting dusty!" he asked.

"That's ok, I'll put out a clean one when he gets here," I answered holding back from crying.

I thought it was so sad that he would ask that question. He was so young and didn't understand the motive behind it. I wiped my hands dry and gave him a tight hug. I had been so busy grieving that I hadn't realized how big little Tyler was getting. He was seven years old and growing like a green bean and still had that toddler innocence about him.

Later that evening, I was preparing to go to bed when the phone began to ring. I ran to answer it, hoping like always that it was Ryan calling.

"Hello?" I answered.

"Hello," said the soft spoken woman.

"Who is this?" I asked.

"It's me, Gina. I just wanted you to know that I just finished having sex with your husband and I can please him better than you," she whispered in a dramatic tone of voice.

I instantly knew who it was and couldn't believe she would call me and tell me such a dreadful thing. Her evil message sent a shockwave of pain through my body dropping me to my knees.

"What you are doing is wrong. It's adultery!" I managed to tell her in between sobs.

"No, it's not," she answered maliciously.

"Yes, it is. It's adultery. He's my husband!" I cried.

"And he's my man," she said venomously.

"You're a devil!" I screamed back slamming the phone down.

Why would she call me and tell me such a wicked thing? My wounds were still fresh and her message did nothing but enhance the pain. I began crying uncontrollably begging God to help me end this nightmare.

"Why Jesus? Why? Why is this happening to me? Why?" I cried while banging my fists against the floor injuring several fingers. I stayed on the floor crying until I finally dragged myself to my closet, and there I prayed in the dark until I calmed down. Later, I climbed into my bed and tried to control the slight whimpers that came from so much crying. I stared at the pillow on Ryan's side of the bed and hungered for his love and embrace.

A few minutes later an inexplicable peacefulness filled the room. I could feel a strong presence in the room hovering over me, but I wasn't afraid. I felt so safe and secure like a small child being soothed to sleep. My entire body was relaxed and my mind was clear.

"Thank you Jesus," I whispered drifting off to sleep.

I slept late the following morning and when I awoke, I thought about last night and the presence of the Lord in my room. I hadn't slept that well since Ryan had left on Christmas morning. Then suddenly, reality struck and I remembered Gina's phone call last night. I could feel the pain in my heart awakening and I began to pray for healing. That same day I started baking homemade bread and went into fasting and prayer.

Everyday, I fasted on bread and liquids alone and prayed for God to reconcile my marriage. After several weeks of fasting, I began losing weight and lots of it. Family members and co-workers started noticing and showed their concern, but I refused to tell anyone that I was fasting.

One night before going to bed, I stood leaning against the closet door staring at Ryan's clothes. I was gently touching the sleeves of his shirts when I noticed my pink plush robe hanging behind his gray one. I took the sleeves from my robe and tied them around the waist of Ryan's robe in an embracing fashion, as if I were hugging him from behind. I smiled at what I had done and went to bed. The following day after work, I was in the parking lot sitting in my truck. I started up the engine and rolled the driver window down an inch or two to allow fresh air into the truck. I was busily searching for a station on the radio when Ryan suddenly appeared and tapped at my window. Startled, I leaned away from the window to look at him. He was peering at me with a serious look on his face and holding some papers close to the window.

"I need to serve you with these papers," he informed me through the crack of the window.

"What are they?" I asked.

"Divorce agreement papers," he said.

"No! no! I won't take them," I yelled.

I was horrified and couldn't believe he actually wanted to serve me with divorce papers.

Then he tried to forcefully shove the papers through the crack of the window. I quickly rolled up the window and backed out the truck accelerating loudly as I drove off and this time leaving him in a cloud of dust.

I looked back and saw him standing in the middle of the parking lot watching me as I drove off. I was so afraid of what he was trying to do. I was crying so heavily that the tears blurred my vision. I couldn't tell if the traffic light before me was red or green. To prevent from having an accident, I parked in another parking lot until I was able to calm myself down.

"Please God, help me! I don't want a divorce, please help me, don't let him do this," I prayed as the tears streamed down my cheeks. A few minutes later, I quickly straightened myself up and looked into the rear view mirror. I was afraid that he might follow me and attempt to serve me again, so I got back on the road and drove home.

Chapter 4

It was a cold February afternoon. The boys and I were visiting Ryan's parents down at their two hundred and forty acre ranch. We sat on the front porch talking and expressing our feelings about Ryan and the other woman. I started crying and began begging them to try and talk Ryan out of wanting a divorce.

Ryan loved his parents very much and I was hoping he would at least listen to them. They both knew my heart was breaking and they did their best to comfort me while encouraging me to pray for a miracle.

Several hours later the sun began to set and the darkness grew. I was concerned about the long drive back home. I waved good-bye to my in-laws and walked over toward the old barn and called out to the boys who were playing nearby. I loaded them up into the truck and before I could start the engine, we heard a rustling sound coming from behind the truck.

"It's dad!" yelled the boys.

I quickly looked back and was surprised to see Ryan closing the toolbox to my truck.

"Ryan! I didn't know you were here. What did you put in my toolbox?" I questioned while jumping out of the truck.

As I walked toward him, he quickly backed away from the truck. Curiously, I slowly opened the lid to the toolbox and I was shocked to see that he had thrown the divorce agreement papers inside. I was hurt and upset at his desperation to divorce me, that he would find the most cheesiest ways to serve me the papers. I quickly pulled them out of the toolbox and turned to look at him. He stood motionless looking at me with a dopey look on his face and not saying a word.

"I can't believe you would leave me and the boys for that horrible woman!" I cried smashing the papers against his chest.

I turned my face away from him and began crying. He stood there lacking compassion as he watched me cry. I walked back to the truck and was slowly climbing back in when the boys yelled.

"Mom! Dad threw something into the toolbox!" I clenched my teeth because I knew what he had done. What upset me more was his lack of respect for the boys. I immediately jumped out of the truck and quickly opened the toolbox and removed the divorce agreement papers. As I turned to look at him, he darted disappearing into the barn with me chasing after him. We both stopped and stood in the middle of the barn looking at each other.

Slowly, I lifted the papers in front of my face and tore them up throwing the pieces on the ground. He didn't say a word and I was appalled at his extremely motionless and silent behavior.

"What has happened to this man?" I thought as I looked at him with compassion. I still loved him and knew I had to do some serious praying for God to break his entrancement. I turned and walked away throwing the last piece of paper at his feet.

Several days later, I received a phone call from Ryan asking me to come over to the apartment, so he could speak to me. I was surprised that he actually called and wanted to see me.

"Why? Are you going to try and serve me with those stupid papers again?" I asked.

"No, you tore them up remember? But I really need you to come over here because we need to talk," he insisted.

Feeling skeptical, I accepted his invitation and left the house leaving my younger daughter Tammy baby sitting the boys.

Once I arrived, I parked my truck next to Ryan's and sat for a few minutes taking in deep breaths to control my anxiety. I wondered what Ryan wanted to see me about and I was hoping he had good news.

"Dear Father, please open Ryan's eyes and give him the wisdom he needs to see that he is making a mistake and send him back home to me. Please bless our marriage and bring us back together again," I prayed.

I took one deep breath and got out of the truck and began walking toward the apartment building. As I approached the stairwell, I stopped and looked up at the apartment where Ryan was staying.

"Maybe I should have worn my bullet proof vest, just in case," I thought to myself with a grin.

I knew Ryan would never hurt me. During the years that we were married he always treated me well and constantly told me that he loved me, but now he was trapped in the web of infidelity and I needed to rescue him. I knocked on the door and waited with anticipation. Ryan answered the door and quickly invited me in holding the screen door open with a nervous smile on his face.

"Hi, come on in," he invited. With hesitation, I cautiously entered looking to see if Gina was around and what Ryan was up to now.

"It's ok, come on in," he assured me.

"Here have a seat," he cordially invited, while directing me to the sofa. Ryan then sat across from me on a lounging chair and stared at me quietly. I could feel the blood rushing to my face as I sat there waiting in suspense.

"What did you want to talk to me about?" I asked. "I'll tell you here in a minute," he answered nervously clearing his throat.

Then the sound of a door opening and shutting down the hallway caught my attention. I was astound to see Gina walking seductively down the hallway, wearing a short black lace skimpy night gown and holding a coffee cup in her hand. She swayed into the living room and slowly sat in a chair next to Ryan's. I couldn't help but notice her big twiggy feet as she sexily tucked them underneath her body.

"Hello Darling," she told him dramatically while ignoring my presence in the room.

I sat stunned at her unpleasant demeanor and disrespect toward me. Ryan looked at me with a crafty smile as if he were enjoying the scenario.

"Hello Dear," he answered her, while looking directly at me.

"Aileen, I just want you to know that I love Gina," he informed me.

My heart stung. It felt as if a straight pin was slowing being pushed into it.

"I thought you loved me," I answered.

"I do love you, but I love Gina too," he said.

"But, darling, you said you loved me, remember?" asked Gina in her famous dramatic tone of voice.

"I do love you, but I love my wife too," he answered her.

"Darling, don't you think that we have a wonderful relationship?" she asked staring at him.

They both sat there looking into each other's eyes. Then he stood up and walked over and knelt down next to her chair. I feared for him as I watched him being drawn into her seductiveness. He was being mesmerized by her eyes.

"Yes, dear we do have a wonderful relationship," he answered in a monotonous tone of voice.

It was a scene that made me sick and I couldn't bear it much longer.

"It's an adulterous relationship!" I yelled breaking their trance.

They both laughed with each other as they looked at me with scorn in their eyes. The knife piercing pain in my heart left my body weak and my legs felt numb. I stood up and looked at them with disgust before running out the door. That night, I prayed and cried in my closet again. I prayed for God to give me strength and to be able to forgive Ryan and Gina for what they were doing.

"Dear God, please forgive me for my sins and help me to forgive Ryan and Gina for what they are doing. Please God break their relationship and reconcile my marriage, please help me God," I prayed tearfully.

I continued fasting daily on bread and liquids and praying constantly for God to break Ryan out of his state of deception and to save our marriage. I kept losing weight and I didn't care how skinny I was getting. Family and friends were highly concerned over my weight loss, but I knew there was power in fasting and prayer and I was not going to give up until God restored my marriage. It was not until that Friday night that I received a phone call from Gina. She spoke to me politely inviting me to come over to her apartment so we could talk about Ryan.

Again, I accepted the invitation and headed over there. Once inside her apartment, she sat on the couch and instructed me to sit next to her. It was the first time that I was able to look at her directly, face to face. The first thing I noticed was her dark oval shaped eyes. She had a fascinating way of fluttering her eyes that gave out an enchanting sparkle and quickly I looked away.

"That's what did it! It was her eyes that got him," I quickly thought to myself.

"I know this must be hard for you, but Ryan loves me," she said trying to be sympathetic.

"No, he loves me," I assured her.

"Ryan and I have been seeing each other for two years and I know he loves me. He wants to marry me and give me a new life," she explained calmly.

"Two years? Marry her? New life?" I thought to myself feeling a hard thump in my heart. I was extremely surprised and couldn't believe what I was hearing.

"No, please you can't. He's my husband. We've been married for nine years and we have children. Please don't do this to us. I don't want a divorce," I pleaded with her. "I'm sorry, but he doesn't love you anymore, he loves me. Besides, I love everything about him, especially the way he wears his hair," she said coldly.

"That's because I cut his hair," I informed her.

"That's not true. He gets his hair cut at the salon," she sneered raising her eyebrows.

"Not this last time. I cut his hair a month ago and he even kissed me three times," I informed her.

"He did what! He kissed you!?" she screamed getting up from the sofa. "It can't be true, he loves me!" she demanded screaming.

She then ran to the telephone and frantically dialed Ryan's cell phone number. Once he answered, she began screaming and demanding an answer about where he last got his haircut. While that was going on, I began praying the "Our Father" under my breath as my heart began beating faster and faster.

Quickly, she interrupted my praying and instructed me to pick up the other telephone in the kitchen, so I could listen to their conversation.

"Darling, please tell me that you love me and not your wife," I heard her ask confidently.

"Yes, I love you dear," he answered.

"Do you still love your wife?" she asked him.

"No, I love you," he assured her. My heart sank at his response and I couldn't believe I was allowing myself to listen to their crazy conversation. Ryan didn't know that I was listening on the other line, so I figured I would just throw a little wood into the fire.

"Ryan, don't you remember when I cut your hair? You kissed me three times and you told me that you loved me," I asked reminding him.

He was silent. Then we both listened as Gina began screaming and cursing at him demanding to know if what I had just said was true.

"This woman is crazy," I thought to myself hanging up the telephone. I could still hear Gina screaming and cursing in the living room. I was alarmed by her behavior and decided it was time to leave. As I began walking out of the living room, I heard her slam the phone hanging up on Ryan. I couldn't help but stare at her as she cried loudly. She looked so pathetic standing there with her arms limp by her side. Her head was tilted back, her face pale as the moon and her mouth wide open as she cried hysterically.

I felt a strong compassion for her. She reminded me of myself when I cried in that same manner when Ryan left me. She had secretly been seeing Ryan for two years and now she was afraid she might lose him. I slowly walked up to her while she was still crying and looked at her. The tears were pouring down her face and her chest was heaving rapidly as she cried. It was only "Jesus" in me that led me to reach out and put my arms around her. I held her close to me and placed her head against my shoulder where she continued to cry.

"It's ok, but please understand that he is my husband," I said gently while trying to soothe her.

When she heard those words she quickly pulled away from me and began screaming even louder. I turned away and quickly ran out the front door. I jumped into my truck and began crying myself. I was afraid, very afraid and I needed God to help ease the pain that was tearing my heart apart. I stayed in my truck praying until I was able to compose myself and drive back home.

Chapter 5

It was early March and two weeks had gone by since my encounters with Ryan and Gina at their apartment. I prayed and fasted obsessively that Ryan would leave Gina and come back home to me. I prayed in the morning, in the afternoon, in the evening and every chance I had. I was desperate! I wanted my husband back home and I was not going to lose faith in the Lord and give up.

One day at work, I was sitting at my desk busily flipping through paperwork when I was dispatched to the sergeant's office. As I entered into the administrative office, I was greeted by Sergeant Rudy Delaney. He extended his hand toward the door and directed me to enter his office. As I entered the office, I was greeted by civil process server, Julian Lamar, who was a very good friend of mine.

"Hi Aileen!" he greeted extending his hand.

"Hi Julian," I answered shaking his hand.

I turned to look at the door as Sergeant Delaney shut it quietly leaving me alone with Julian.

"So? What's going on Julian?" I asked quietly.

"I'm sorry, but I have to serve you with these papers," he said compassionately.

I looked down and stared at the divorce agreement papers he was holding in his hand.

"No, I don't want them, no!" I said frantically, hearing my heartbeat as it pounded against my chest.

Julian then held me in his arms and comforted me while I cried on his shoulder.

"No Julian, I don't want a divorce. He left me for another woman and that's why he's doing this. Please, I don't want those papers," I pleaded.

"I know and I understand. But I have to serve you," he sympathized while handing me the divorce papers.

Feeling defeated, I took the papers from his hand and held them limp by my side without looking at them.

"Ryan finally got me," I thought to myself. My body felt heavy as if the gravity was forcefully trying to pull me down to my knees. I felt faint and I didn't care if I dropped dead on the floor. I didn't want these papers and I didn't want a divorce. My life with Ryan flashed before me as my world came crashing down.

The papers felt like lead in my left hand as I walked out of the office and into the hallway. My shoulders were slumped and my head was hanging low. My left shoulder was rubbing along the wall as I staggered down the hallway. The humiliation was minor compared to the crushing pain in my chest.

I was disoriented and went into a state of tunnel vision. I remember only seeing the brown carpet at my feet and the blur of blue police uniforms slowly moving out of my way as I walked past them. I definitely was the center of attention and I knew that everyone was watching me as I came down the hallway.

I turned left at the end of the hallway and entered into the women's restroom to hide myself from the officers and the rest of the world. I slammed the door behind me and placed my forehead against the wall and began crying. Angelina, the housekeeper was inside the restroom cleaning. She was a slender middle aged woman with blue eyes and fine features. Her long gray hair was neatly braided and wrapped in a bun behind her head.

I felt her gently removing the papers from my hand. After she recognized what they were, she put her arm around my shoulders and hugged me snuggly against her chest to comfort me.

While I was crying, she began to whimper softly. Through tearful eyes, I curiously looked at Angelina wondering why she was crying too. Angelina then slowly began wiping the tears from her eyes.

"I'm so sorry," she said sadly.

"Angelina, why are *you* crying?" I asked sobbingly.

"I caught my husband having an affair with my sister and I too am going through a divorce," she whispered in between sobs.

"Your sister?" I asked sounding surprised.

She nodded her head and began crying again. I felt sorrowful not just for myself, but for her and all the others out there who were going through the same tragedy this very moment. I hugged her and gently comforted her as she cried on my shoulder.

"Why God? Why are there so many divorces? Why can't husbands and wives be faithful and love one another?" I asked the Lord in my mind as a single tear finished rolling down my cheek.

A few minutes later, I left the restroom and walked outside the building and hid in a corner. My eyes froze with horror as I began reading the first page of the divorce agreement papers which were filed in the 143rd District Court.

"No! This can't be happening. Ryan is actually trying to divorce me," I thought as I continued reading.

I frantically ran back into the building and up to the second floor. I walked into the 143rd District Court and desperately began searching each office hoping to find Judge Ellen Renner. I wanted to beg her not to grant the divorce that Ryan so eagerly wanted. After discovering that she was not in her chambers, I quickly ran out into the long hallway desperately looking up and down hoping to find the judge.

I was deeply despaired with the terrifying thought of Ryan divorcing me for another woman. I had to stop him and I needed someone to help me. I felt that time was running out and I couldn't wait for Judge Renner much longer, so I ran down the stairs and out of the building. I stood still, desperately watching the world of traffic and people moving about in the streets and sidewalks. I remember people walking by glancing at me with curious looks on their faces.

Then I noticed the steeple of a church one block away from where I was standing. I bolted and began running toward the church with bystanders watching me as I ran past them. Then I realized that I was in full uniform and that I was probably giving people the impression that I was answering a call at the church.

I slowed down as I approached the large wooden doors and stepped inside. I looked around at the few people who were quietly praying. Without hesitation, I ran toward the back of the huge alter searching the back rooms for a priest. The young receptionist sat curiously looking at me as I approached her desk.

"I need to speak to a priest," I said with desperation in my voice.

"There are no priests right now. They're all out at a convention," she explained politely.

"Thank you," I said quickly walking out of the office. I was panic stricken and ran out through the side door of the church and into the parking lot. I stood outside in despair, not realizing that I was wringing the divorce papers between my hands. I didn't know where else to go. I felt abandoned and alone. There was no one else around to turn to for help. I wanted so desperately to talk to someone, but who? Who can help me ease the suffering and the pain that I was experiencing this very moment? Who could restore my broken spirit and make things new again? Who could make this nightmare go away?

"Somebody please help me," I whispered.

I stood there looking pitiful as the wind briskly blew through my hair. I turned to look as the wind forcefully swung the church door open almost striking it against the building's wall. I could clearly see the alter through the open door. I felt drawn toward it, as if it were inviting me inside. I slowly walked through the door and quietly made my way up to the alter.

Broken in spirit and with a tear stained face, I fell to my knees and began praying for a miracle.

It was then that I came to realize how much God really loved me. While I was frantically running around searching for the judge and a priest, God waited patiently for me to come to Him. I asked for forgiveness and decided to trust God with whatever else was yet to come. Then my police radio began to transmit loudly, echoing through out the sanctuary breaking the silence. I was being dispatched to the sergeant's office again. I never returned to my post and they were looking for me. I pathetically walked into the sergeant's office still holding the divorce papers in my hand. My head was hanging low as I stood before Sgt. Delaney. He took one good look at me and instructed me to take the next couple of days off.

As I drove back home, I was flipping through the stations on the radio when I decided to listen to Pastor Ricky Calvert preach. He ended his sermon by inviting all those with broken spirits to attend Sunday services at his church. I made it a point to attend services the following Sunday with the boys. I soon learned that morning that Pastor Calvert's wife, Rita Calvert, was a marriage counselor and was known to successfully help in restoring marriages through prayer. I called her office Monday morning and scheduled an appointment for the following day.

Chapter 6

I sat quietly in Rita Calvert's office waiting for her to return from the women's prayer group. Her office was simple with a few green plants near the doorway. Picture frames of family members and grandchildren decorated the shelves. Her desk was neatly organized with a few books piled to one side. A large Holy Bible with a withered maroon cover sat on the middle of the desk.

The door swings open and an elderly woman steps in with a huge smile across her face. Her body appeared thin and fragile in the long blue flowered printed dress and dainty white sweater that she wore. Her gray hair, she wore briskly piled on top of her head and her glasses looked huge against her delicate features.

"Hello, I am Rita Calvert and I am so glad to meet you," she said, reaching out to shake my hand.

"Hi, I'm Aileen Christine Stinson," I answered.

"Aileen? Oh, that is such a beautiful name," she complimented.

"Thank you," I answered.

"So, what brings you here today child?" she asked softly. She was so kind. I had been hurting for so long that just a spark of kindness would start me crying again. I could feel the tears starting to form in my eyes and I was trying my best not to cry. I couldn't answer her question. My throat was locked with pain and trying to swallow made it hurt even more. Then suddenly the reality of Ryan trying to divorce me for another woman struck me harder than ever. I brought my hands up to my face and began crying. "My…husband…left…me," I said forcing the words out.

"Oh, dear child. Was it for another woman?" she asked compassionately.

Instead of answering her, I just nodded my head. I felt angry at myself for crying and struck my right thigh with my fist. I was tired of the crying. I wanted to be strong and able to discuss my situation without the tears.

"Oh, dear child. Don't cry," she said gently as she removed my hands from my face.

"Here, let's pray," she said, cupping her hands around mine.

"Dear Father we come before you and seek your forgiveness for our sins. We also know that you are a loving and merciful God and that you love your children very much. We are asking for you to please heal Aileen's broken heart and renew her spirit. Please give her the strength that she needs to trust you during her time of trouble, and that she can give you all the glory. In Jesus name, Amen."

"Now! Let me ask you a question before we begin," she said leaning back into her chair.

"Ok," I answered softly.

"Do you want to serve the Lord with all your heart? Or, do you want to save your marriage?" she asked leaning slightly forward to hear my answer.

"DO YOU WANT TO SAVE YOUR MARRIAGE?" The words rang so loud in my head

that I forgot the first question. I looked at her with desperation and quickly answered,

"I want to save my marriage!"

She sighed and then leaned back into her chair as if she were dissatisfied with my answer. I was slightly confused and not sure what her reaction meant.

"Ok, so you want to save your marriage, right? Then you will have to start reading," she said handing me a popular book about how to save one's marriage.

"The first thing that we need to do is pray for the Lord to break up your husband's relationship with the other woman," she explained.

After we finished praying, she comforted me once more and invited me to come visit her as often as I needed, until God could bring me an answer.

I left her office feeling strange about something I couldn't pin point. Although my spirit was renewed and my confidence lifted, I felt guilty for some reason. As I walked back to my truck, I could feel a sense of sadness in the air, so I quickly extinguished the feeling because I didn't want to cry again.

As I was driving back home, I was listening to a local Christian radio station. The prayer session I shared with the Pastor's wife lifted my spirit and gave me a sense of hope. I knew God would heal my marriage and send Ryan back home soon. I felt so much better that I actually started to smile again and began singing along to some of the Christian songs on the radio.

As I approached the driveway to the house, I drove up to the mailbox and pulled out the mail. There were several bills and one large brown clasp envelope with my name scribbled sloppily across the top. The envelope was bulky and whoever sent it failed to put a return address. I parked the truck and hurried into the house. I laid the rest of the mail on the table and slowly opened the large brown envelope and looked inside. Startled, I turned the envelope upside down and emptied out the contents. I couldn't believe what my eyes were seeing. It was the photos from the photo album I had placed in Ryan's truck several weeks ago.

My heart sank and my vision blurred as the tears began rapidly forming in my eyes. I sadly searched through the photos trying to be strong and not wanting to cry. The pink heart shaped piece of paper that I had placed in the album was torn into four pieces. I carefully puzzled the pink pieces of paper together and stared at the words; "We love you. Please come home."

"How could they be so cruel? Was this Ryan's evil work or the other woman's?" I wondered, as I began placing all the photos back into the envelope.

I then scribbled the words; "I forgive you" across the top. Less than an hour ago my spirit was lifted and now it was crushed again. I laid in bed forcing myself not to cry.

"No more crying!" I whispered to myself.

"NO MORE CRYING!" I demanded loudly as a few tear drops trickled onto my pillow. I then silently prayed to God for strength and fell asleep.

Chapter 7

A few days after I had received the photos in the mail, I called Rita Calvert's office and scheduled an appointment to see her the following week. I had grieved for two days over the photos and longed for her to pray with me.

Later that afternoon, I was strolling around outside the ranch enjoying the beauty of the day. I walked up to the old wooden corral that surrounded the barn and leaned my arms over the top of it. The fresh country air smelled so good that it seemed to ease away some of my depression. It was early March and a few spring flowers were starting to bloom. It reminded me that soon the entire field would be blanketed with wildflowers.

As I looked around at the acreage, I noticed how empty the pastures looked without the cattle roaming and grazing about. Ryan had transferred the cattle to his father's ranch several weeks before leaving.

"He had it all planned out," I thought sadly. And now, the pastures had grown tall and brushy.

My heart was aching and I felt lonely. I wanted Ryan back. Why would he break up our family and force me to become a single parent to raise our sons alone, just for another woman. Family members and friends constantly advised me to leave the situation in God's hands and to wait. But, how easier said than done. Waiting is not that easy when you are the victim dealing with rejection.

I looked up to the sky hoping I could see a glimpse of the Lord's face between the clouds. I called out to the Lord and began praying.

"Lord, please lift me up. I don't want to hurt anymore. Please heal my broken heart. Help me to be strong as I wait for Ryan to come back home. Thank you Lord." I then ended with a special prayer for Ryan and the children.

A few minutes later, I was beginning to feel better, much better. I started humming to myself as I walked down the long sandy driveway to check the mailbox. Prayer always seemed to renew my spirit and I was feeling confident that it would be a matter of time before Ryan would come home.

I opened the mailbox and removed the mail. I was flipping through the bills when I came across a white envelope, again with my name sloppily scribbled across it. My hands froze as I held the envelope. The handwriting was identical to the writing on the large brown envelope that had the photos in it.

Feeling uneasy about the letter, I slowly walked back to the house and sat on the porch steps. My hands were shaking as I opened the envelope. I removed the letter that had two enclosed photos of our ranch and I began to read;

To Aileen, I am sending you these photos of your ranch that Ryan had in his bag. He will not be needing them. I thought that maybe these photos could help comfort you during your time of dilemma. I just wanted you to know that Ryan does not want you anymore. He wants me. We are very much in love with each other. We are so happily in love that we feel like teenagers all over again. Well, good luck to you old lady! Gina.

My hands became limp and the letter fell to the ground. I closed my eyes and bit my lower lip. I bit it so hard that I didn't care if it bled. I held my breath. I didn't want to cry. I could feel my body shaking as I tried to be strong. No matter how hard I tried not to cry, the tears still forced their way out and down my cheeks.

I felt angry at them for torturing me. I didn't want to cry! I quickly wiped the tears off my face and stood up from the porch steps. I stared down at the letter lying on the ground. I wanted to get rid of it. I thought about sending it back to Gina, but that would have been too easy. I had a better plan. I picked up the letter and walked back into the house. I searched the kitchen drawers until I found a box of matches and headed out to the barn. I opened the gate to the corral and began digging a hole in the sand. I took the letter and read it once more and prayed;

"Father, I lift this letter up to you that you may deal with it according to your purposes and for your Glory. In Jesus' name, Amen."

I then tore the letter into little pieces and threw them into the hole. I lit a match and stared at the flame for a few seconds and then tossed it into the hole, setting the pieces on fire. I prayed silently as the pieces burned and watched as the ashes and smoke twirled with the breeze.

Then I prayed for strength to forgive Gina for sending me the letter and her evil intentions behind it. I stood watching the fire until the very last piece had finished burning. My heart was numb, it had taken enough beating and I was exhausted.

I walked away from the smoldering fire and went into the barn. The heartache was coming back. It started nibbling at me again and at the same time robbing me of my strength. I didn't want to be defeated and through the power of perseverance and faith, I knew I could win. I fell on the ground burying my knees in the sand and began praying again. After a few moments of intense prayer, I opened my eyes and I couldn't believe what I was seeing. There was a beautiful red bird perched on the gate very close to me. And there were hundreds of sparrows joining the red bird, perching themselves next to it and all along the corral. There were numerous butterflies touching down on the wildflowers nearby. I was amazed at the huge yellow sunbeam that spotlighted the green fields next to the barn.

The colors appeared enhanced and the air seemed so fresh and cool. I stood up in awe and looked at my surroundings. It was all so beautiful.

"Oh God, I love you. It's all so beautiful. Thank you," I said temporarily forgetting my pain.

Somehow, I felt confident that everything was going to be alright.

"Ryan is just going through a phase. He will be back home soon," I convinced myself.

I held onto my faith and my spirit was lifted once more. Until one week later when I discovered I was wrong. I received a letter informing me that my divorce hearing was scheduled for April 24th at nine o'clock in the morning. I almost passed out as I read the fine print. I felt nauseous. My mind was swirling and I had to lie down on my bed. I cried silently. I didn't want a divorce.

"Why God? Why haven't you helped me? Why are you allowing this to happen to me?" I cried out.

I knew not to question God and quickly asked for forgiveness. I laid in bed for hours thinking about Ryan and how he fell prey into the other woman's seductiveness. He was living in a fantasy world and was experiencing some sort of temporary insanity. I had to keep praying for God to open his eyes. Maybe Ryan would cancel the divorce proceedings. I had to beat this nightmare, so I began fasting daily, strictly on bread and liquids once again.

Chapter 8

After several days of fasting, I received a phone call from Ryan. He began intimidating me that he had retained two good attorneys and was determined to sell the ranch. Shocked, I cried and pleaded with Ryan not to sell the ranch.

"No, first you leave me for another woman and now you want to take my home away?" I cried.

"I suggest you get yourself a good lawyer," he sneered cold heartedly before hanging up on me.

I panicked and called Rita Calvert's office and asked if I could see her right away. Once in her office, I broke down and cried hysterically explaining my situation to her.

"Here, call this attorney. Her name is Darlene Zamora. She is a good Christian woman and she can help you," she said, comforting me.

I took the piece of paper with the attorney's name on it and immediately called her office and scheduled an appointment for the next day.

I was thirty minutes early for my appointment with Darlene Zamora. I sat patiently in her office watching her as she finished shuffling through the paperwork on her desk.

"Ok, how can I help you?" she asked.

"My husband left me for another woman. He hired two attorneys and filed for divorce," I told her.

"Ok, I will have to contact his attorneys and then we can work out an agreement," she said.

"No! You don't understand. I don't want a divorce. Please don't let it go through. I need to fight it," I said anxiously.

"Ok, then I will need at least six hundred and forty dollars to start," she said. I almost fell out of my chair. *"Six hundred and forty dollars?"* I thought to myself.

"I don't have that kind of money," I told her.

"Then I can't handle your case," she said bluntly.

I was stunned. I couldn't believe she was turning me away. I put my head down on her desk and began sobbing. I didn't care about my dignity anymore. I lost it when Ryan left me. Then I felt her gently touching my hair, asking me to pick up my head. She held my hands and began to pray with me. After she prayed over me, she escorted me out the door and informed me that she would pray for God to help me find the right attorney. I whimpered softly as I walked away from her office.

Now what? I had to find another attorney. As soon as I got home, I began searching through the phone book and came across an Edwin Chapman who advertised himself as being a Christian attorney with reasonable rates. I quickly dialed the number and made an appointment for the following day.

The next day, I arrived at his office a few minutes early and sat in the waiting room feeling nervous.

"Maybe this one will help me," I thought to myself.

I knew it was going to cost money to have an attorney represent me. But I was hoping to find one who would agree to a payment plan.

"God, please let this attorney help me. Let him be the one I need to handle my case. Please God, I don't want a divorce," I prayed as I waited.

"Aileen Christine? Hi, I'm Edwin Chapman. Please come into my office," he said directing me through the door.

I sat in the large maroon leather chair in front of his desk. He sat down behind his desk and looked at me for a few seconds. I knew he was looking at my face which showed signs of stress. I had bags and small hairline wrinkles forming underneath my eyes from so much crying. "Ok, so what brings you here today?" he asked, sitting back swinging conceitedly in his huge black leather chair.

"My husband has filed for divorce. He left me for another woman and I need you to help me stop the divorce proceedings," I said pleadingly.

"Well, first thing's first. Let me go ahead and discuss my fees with you. I will need seven hundred down to start your case," he informed me.

"Seven hundred!" I thought disappointedly.

"Can't you put me on a payment plan?" I asked.

"I'm sorry. But I can't do that. I need seven hundred down before I can even start working on your case," he said.

"I don't have the money," I told him.

"Then I can't help you," he said.

I felt so rejected. It was all about money. None of these attorneys cared enough to help put me on a payment plan. My divorce hearing was next month and I was being rejected again. I looked at him with disappointment in my eyes and began to cry. I cried for several minutes and then realized that this attorney had no compassion at all. At least Darlene Zamora stroked my hair and prayed with me. I looked up at him. He was rocking back and forth in his big fancy chair quietly watching me.

"Are you a Christian?" I asked him.

"Uh, yes I am," he said.

"I don't think so!" I said rudely as I got up and ran out of his office.

I sat in my truck with my forehead leaning against the steering wheel. I felt guilty criticizing the attorney the way I did. He was immune to my feelings and I was just another statistic in his book.

"What am I going to do God? What am I going to do?" I repeatedly asked myself as I watched the tears drip down onto my lap. I couldn't afford an attorney and I couldn't give up. I had to keep on looking. Time was running out. Since I worked at the courthouse, I began asking around if anyone knew of a good attorney that was reasonable in price. The thought of Ryan hiring two attorneys worried me. He was serious about selling the ranch and splitting everything we had down the middle. Totally wiping me out of home and marriage. As well as forcing the boys to come from a broken home.

It was the first week in April and my divorce hearing was just three weeks away. One afternoon, I was sitting on a park bench outside the courthouse when a female attorney approached me.

"Hi, my name is Jean Glenmore, someone told me that you were looking for an attorney," she said extending her hand out to me.

I shook her hand and we spoke briefly about my situation. I then agreed to meet at her office at five thirty that afternoon. I sat in her office that afternoon explaining my situation when the phone rang. She excused herself and answered the phone. I couldn't help but listen to her conversation. I could tell that the voice on the other end of the phone was a woman. She sounded frantic and Jean was speaking harshly toward her trying to get her to calm down. She kept sympathizing with the woman and then agreed to meet with her the following day. She hung up the phone and then rolled her eyes and shook her head with frustration.

"I'm sorry about that," she said apologetically.

"Oh, that's ok," I answered.

"The woman I just spoke to was diagnosed with breast cancer and her husband left her for another woman and she is going absolutely crazy," she grumbled.

I couldn't believe how insensitive she was. I felt heavy-hearted for the other woman. She had breast cancer. Her situation was worse than mine. I thought about her pain and suffering and didn't realize that my head was hanging low.

"Are you going to be ok?" asked Jean.

"Yes, ma'am," I said sadly.

"Well, I am going to need six hundred and fifty dollars to get your case started. I will contact your husband's attorneys and then we will go from there," she said sternly while shuffling paperwork on her desk.

I slowly looked up at her and realized that I didn't want this woman to represent me, money or no money.

"I'm sorry but I can't afford to hire you. Thank you for your time," I told her and then exited her office. I walked back to my truck and sat for at least fifteen minutes thinking about my life and what was to become of me and the boys. I gripped the steering wheel tight as I fought the tears that tried to force their way out. As much as I didn't want to cry, a few tears still managed to escape and trickle down my cheeks. I wiped my eyes dry and headed back home.

It was the third week in April and I still wasn't able to find a reasonable attorney. It was Friday; the end of the work week and somehow I managed to pull through the day. I spent most of the day in a zombie state of mind and wasn't talking much with my co-workers. I prayed silently, keeping to myself. Ryan was divorcing me for another woman and in just five short days my whole life was going to change dramatically. The thought of losing everything; my husband, marriage, home and future all destroyed because of his lust for another woman. I couldn't understand it.

As much praying and fasting that I did, I was not sure why God had not reconciled my marriage. At this point, I didn't care anymore. I wasn't going to question God and I knew I had to trust Him. I needed

Him to touch my life and to help me somehow make it through the next five days. I stopped worrying about trying to find an attorney and whatever else was at stake. I continued to fast and prayed for a miracle. Being that it was slow that afternoon, I decided to do a little foot patrol through out the courthouse. A short while later, I was on the second floor waiting for the elevator. I was in deep thought about Ryan and Gina when I heard a familiar voice call out to me.

"Hello Officer Stinson!" I turned around and was surprised to see that it was Mr. Noel Fazio.

"Oh! Hello Mr. Fazio," I answered.

He eagerly shook my hand and began examining my face.

"Hey, what's with the long face?" he asked cupping my chin with his hand.

"Mr. Fazio my husband left me for another woman and now he filed for divorce. He wants to sell our ranch and everything. My hearing is next week and I still can't find a reasonable attorney," I explained.

"Why didn't you call me?" he asked kindly.

"Mr. Fazio, I can't hire you. You run a million dollar law firm," I said.

"Well, you know what? I won't charge you a dime," he said with a big smile on his face.

"Oh my God! Are you serious?" I asked delightfully.

"Hey! What are friends for? You arrested me remember?" he said playfully extending his wrists out to me.

"Come on, let's go down to the cafeteria. I'll buy you a cup of coffee and we can talk," he invited.

As I walked with Mr. Fazio, I kept thanking God under my breath. God came through for me again and this time bringing me a bigger miracle. A free attorney. And of all attorneys, it was the one that I had arrested for unlawfully carrying a weapon. I couldn't believe it. Only God works in mysterious ways. God had it all so carefully planned out. Praise my Lord!

Chapter 9

Here it was. The final court date hearing. I sat in the back row of the 143rd District Court. I nervously looked around and didn't see Ryan anywhere in the courtroom. Our hearing was at nine o'clock and he still hadn't shown up. A few minutes later Mr. Fazio's assistant, Mrs. Maria Shapiro arrived and explained to me that she was instructed by Mr. Fazio to represent me since he was due in court that morning.

"Where's Ryan?" I asked her.

"Oh, he's not coming. I was told that he was hung over from a divorce party he attended last night," she whispered.

"What? He was celebrating our divorce?" I asked her with disbelief.

"Yea, you don't need a man like that," she said.

I was hurt. On top of everything else and he still had to go celebrate our divorce. Thoughts of him and Gina drinking and laughing it up, tore at my heart. It was all so wrong. I felt stripped, dumped, and rejected. But above all the pain and suffering I was experiencing that morning, and as crazy as it may sound, I still loved him and wanted him back home. I wanted to save our marriage and be a family again for the boys' sake. But looking back at all what I went through in the past few months, deep down inside me, I knew it would never work out. There would always be friction in our relationship. Even if I forgave him, the memories would still haunt my mind and heart.

Mrs. Shapiro then went over the divorce papers with me. She informed me that Mr. Fazio had contacted Ryan's attorneys and they convinced Ryan to give me everything. Ryan lost everything in the divorce and was only allowed to keep his retirement. As I stood before the bench with Mrs. Shapiro, I was beginning to feel faint. My face was flushing as the reality of the divorce began unfolding before my very eyes.

My ears felt hot and I could barely hear what Judge Renner was saying. Judge Renner was awarding me the ranch house, acreage, furniture, truck and everything else, except for Ryan's retirement. I stood motionless as I listened with my face drawn only nodding my head in agreement. Then I looked up and saw Judge Renner raise the gavel up high above her head. I knew if she struck the gavel it would be all over. I panicked and quickly interrupted,

"Judge! I don't want a divorce. I love my husband and we have two sons," I begged.

Judge Renner continued holding the gavel in the air and took one long look at Mrs. Shapiro.

"Mrs. Shapiro, I suggest you take your client into the jury room and confer with her about this matter. Court is in recess," said Judge Renner striking the gavel and stepping down from the bench. I followed Mrs. Shapiro into the jury room and began crying.

"I know the Judge is awarding me with everything, but I don't want a divorce," I cried. "I need to call a priest," I insisted reaching for the phone.

"What for?" she asked removing the phone from my hand. "All you need to do is trust God. I know you don't want a divorce, but God has a special plan for you. Something good comes from something bad and one day you'll discover what it is," she said encouraging me.

Mrs. Shapiro then took my hands and began praying for God to give me peace, comfort and joy, as well as strength to withstand the divorce hearing.

"Are you ready now?" she asked softly.

"Yes, let's get it over with," I said wiping my eyes.

We stood before the bench once more. Judge Renner then read over the conditions and asked if I agreed. "Yes," I answered.

Then the sound of the gavel came crashing down on the platform. What was suppose to be sacred was instantly sacrificed to a god other than the Almighty God I served.

"Divorce granted!" said Judge Renner.

It was over. I stood there surprised that I didn't lose control and break down crying. Suddenly, I felt sensationally strong as the tremendous amount of pressure was lifted from me. The burden was gone and I felt free. The happiness in my heart was restored and I never felt so joyful in my life. The divorce was final. And the tribulation was over. Now I felt sad for Ryan. I knew that he had chosen the wrong path in life and there was nothing else I could do but pray for him.

I drove back home in a daze as I thought about Jesus and how He helped me through my time of adversity. Jesus was always there to comfort me when

I cried and to carry me through the most difficult times. I thought about how He answered my prayers revealing Ryan and Gina's affair. I thought about His presence in my room that one night. I thought about the dark skinned woman who guided me. I thought about how He revealed himself in the beauty of His creation reminding me that He was near. I thought about how He called me to the alter when I was desperate. I thought about the miracle in receiving a free attorney right before the hearing. Then…I thought about why He didn't reconcile my marriage. While lingering on the thought, a flashback of Rita Calvert's question flashed across my mind.

"Do you want to serve the Lord with all your heart? Or, do you want to save your marriage?"

I suddenly realized that I had made the wrong choice. I had placed my Lord last just to save my marriage. My obsession in getting Ryan back became an idol before the Lord, and I proved it by making the wrong choice. I know now that I should have chosen to serve my Lord first and then pray for reconciliation. Some people have argued the case, but deep down in my heart I believe I simply made the wrong choice. I asked God for forgiveness and vowed to always place Him first in my life.

I pulled into the driveway and got out of the truck. It was a beautiful spring day. I stood in the driveway looking around at all what God had blessed me with. The big ranch house with its four huge oak trees in front and the climbing roses blooming along the deck and fence lines. The twelve acres of land filled with colorful wildflowers. And one red bird perched on the gate. It was all so beautiful and God had given me sole ownership of it all. This is my story.

Conclusion

This book is to be made available to the general population as well as to the Christian Community. I lift this book up to God for His purposes and for His Glory and that it may lift up those who are experiencing the effects of rejection and divorce. "Is he?" I constantly asked myself wondering if Ryan was having an affair. But now, I ask myself, "Is He? Is God Almighty the Lord over my life?" Yes, He is. May God be with you during your time of trouble and lead you to victory.

About the Author

The author, a current police officer of twelve years, has always found herself helping her comrades by listening and comforting them during their troubled marriages and divorces. Not knowing, that someday she would be going through the same difficult episode herself. Refusing to become another statistic in the high divorce rate among police officers, she desperately fought to save her marriage. Although she endured a tragic divorce, she continues to comfort, teach and share her experiences with other troubled couples in the police force. The constant replaying in her mind of her husband's betrayal led her to write her first book.